The Bobwhite and Other Quail Of The United States

by Sylvester D. Judd

with an introduction by Jackson Chambers

This work contains material that was originally published in 1905.

This publication is within the Public Domain.

This edition is reprinted for educational purposes
and in accordance with all applicable Federal Laws.

Introduction Copyright 2018 by Jackson Chambers

Self Reliance Books

Get more historic titles on animal and stock breeding, gardening and old fashioned skills by visiting us at:

http://selfreliancebooks.blogspot.com/

Introduction

I am pleased to present yet another title on Raising Quail.

This volume is entitled "Quailology" and was published by Fred Kerr in 1903.

The work is in the Public Domain and is re-printed here in accordance with Federal Laws.

As with all reprinted books of this age that are intended to perfectly reproduce the original edition, considerable pains and effort had to be undertaken to correct fading and sometimes outright damage to existing proofs of this title. At times, this task is quite monumental, requiring an almost total "rebuilding" of some pages from digital proofs of multiple copies. Despite this, imperfections still sometimes exist in the final proof and may detract from the visual appearance of the text.

I hope you enjoy reading this book as much as I enjoyed making it available to readers again.

Jackson Chambers

BOBWHITE IN POTATO FIELD.

LETTER OF TRANSMITTAL.

U. S. DEPARTMENT OF AGRICULTURE,
BIOLOGICAL SURVEY,
Washington, D. C., July 31, 1905.

SIR: I have the honor to transmit herewith, for publication as Bulletin 21 of the Biological Survey, a report on the quails of the United States and their economic value, by Sylvester D. Judd. The quails as a group are perhaps better known through the country than any other birds. From the time of the first settlements in New England and Virginia till the present day they have been favorite objects of pursuit by sportsmen, and are widely known as table delicacies.

The chief purpose of the present paper is to consider the quails in their economic relations to the farmer—relations not so well understood as they deserve to be. Investigation shows the birds to be no less important in their economic than in their other relations to man. They are found to be exceedingly valuable allies of agriculture because of the quantity of noxious insects and weed seeds they destroy, while the harm they do is insignificant.

I am indebted to my assistant, E. W. Nelson, for preparing the introduction and critically reading the text, and to the Bureau of Entomology for the identification of many of the insects mentioned.

Respectfully,

C. HART MERRIAM,
Chief Biological Survey.

Hon. JAMES WILSON,
Secretary of Agriculture.

CONTENTS.

	Page.
Introduction	7
The bobwhite (*Colinus virginianus*)	9
Call notes	10
Breeding habits	11
General habits	13
Bobwhite as an ally of the farmer	14
Bobwhite as an asset of the farm	15
Bobwhite as an article of food	16
Bobwhite as an object of sport	16
Esthetic value of bobwhite	17
Decrease of bobwhite	18
Legislation in behalf of bobwhite	19
Measures for preservation and propagation	20
Food habits	27
Grain as food	28
Weed seeds as food	31
List of weed seeds eaten	34
Mast and pine seeds as food	35
Fruit as food	35
List of fruits eaten	37
Leaves and buds as food	37
Insects as food	37
Beetles eaten	38
List of beetles eaten	41
Bugs eaten	42
List of bugs eaten	42
Grasshoppers and allied insects eaten	43
Caterpillars eaten	44
List of caterpillars eaten	45
Miscellaneous animal food	45
Food of the young	45
Masked bobwhite (*Colinus ridgwayi*)	46
California quail (*Lophortyx californicus*)	47
Food habits	49
Insect and other animal food	49
Vegetable food	50
Fruit	50
Grain	51
Leaves	52
Weed seeds	52
Food of the young	55
Gambel quail (*Lophortyx gambeli*)	56
Food habits	57
Mountain quail (*Oreortyx pictus*)	58
Food habits	59
Scaled quail (*Callipepla squamata*)	61
Food habits	61
Mearns quail (*Cyrtonyx montezumæ mearnsi*)	63
Food habits	63

LIST OF ILLUSTRATIONS.

PLATES.

Page.

PLATE I. Bobwhite .... Frontispiece.
    II. Gambel quail 56

TEXT FIGURES.

FIG. 1. Witch grass seed 31
    2. Crab grass seed 32
    3. Knot grass seed 33
    4. Mayweed seed 53
    5. Alfilaria seed 53
    6. Black mustard seed 53
    7. Chickweed seed 54
    8. Geranium seed 54
    9. Sorrel seed 54
    10. Chess seed 55

THE BOBWHITE AND OTHER QUAILS OF THE UNITED STATES IN THEIR ECONOMIC RELATIONS.

INTRODUCTION.

The quails of the United States, because of their interesting habits and marvelous diversity of form and color, are a notably attractive group. All are handsome birds, but the most striking and beautiful species live in the Southwest and on the Pacific coast. Seven species occur within our borders, but only one in the Eastern States. The others are widely distributed from Texas to California and Oregon. Their range was, and still is, continuous along the entire southern border of the country from the Atlantic to the Pacific; but there is an irregular belt along the northern border and a large area in the interior, comprising the Great Plains, the northern three-fourths of the Great Basin, and the Rocky Mountains, in which they appear to have been originally wanting.

With few exceptions our quails welcome the extension of agriculture, and the added food supply in farmed areas results in an increase of their numbers. This is equally true of the bobwhite of the East, and of some of the desert species of the West. So fully does the bobwhite appreciate the advantages of the farm that its range has increased with the extension of the cultivated area, especially west of the Mississippi.

The quails, because of their cheerful habits, their beauty, and their value as food, are usually welcome on the farm; but their real value to agriculture is not yet generally understood. The investigations of the Biological Survey show that these birds, with rare exceptions, are not only harmless, but that usually they are very useful to agriculture. This is particularly true of the bobwhite, which constantly feeds on injurious weed seeds and insects, and thus renders valuable service to the farmer. In return for this good service it is but fair that these birds should be treated with friendly care and interest.

The well-known bobwhite is the only quail indigenous to the Eastern United States, where it ranges from southern New England to Florida and Texas; but owing to climatic influences the birds of Florida and of Texas differ enough to be distinguished as geographic races. Wherever it occurs, however, the bobwhite has the same call, and varies but little in habits. A closely related bird, the masked bobwhite, inhabited southern Arizona until within a few years. Owing to dry seasons and the overstocking of its home with cattle, this bird is now supposed to be extinct within our borders; but some probably exist in parts of Sonora, Mexico.

Although bobwhites are handsome birds, yet they are the plainest quail in the United States except the ' cotton top ' or scaled quail of the deserts of southern Texas and Arizona. The latter is slaty bluish on the upper parts, which are ornamented with large scale-like markings, and has a whitish crest.

The most bizarre and curious of all is the Mearns quail of the high, broken plains and mountain slopes of southwestern Texas, southern New Mexico and Arizona. It is short and round bodied, like a little guinea hen, and this superficial likeness is increased by brilliant round white spots ornamenting the dark sides. It is the gentlest of all the quails and is so unsuspicious that when a person encounters one it often walks unconcernedly about or stands looking curiously at the newcomer, when it is not infrequently killed with a stick or stone, a characteristic which, among the people where it lives, has earned for it the name of ' Fool Quail.'

The Gambel quail is a habitant of the southwestern desert region, where it ranges the brushy foothills and the valleys along water-courses. It is a beautiful bird, the head handsomely marked and adorned with a jet-black recurving crest, and the flanks bright chestnut, brilliantly streaked with white. This quail, one of the most conspicuous and pleasing forms of desert life, is numerous wherever it can find sufficient food and water. For ages it has claimed many a remote watering place as its own, but it welcomes the settler and finds additional shelter and food in his irrigated fields. Under the new conditions its numbers increase and it repays the favors received by becoming semidomesticated. Its presence adds a touch of bright color and animation to the dreary surroundings of many a lonely desert ranch.

The California valley quail belongs entirely to the Pacific coast, and probably is the most beautiful of the smaller gallinaceous birds of the world. It resembles the Gambel quail in its recurving black crest and general appearance, but exceeds that bird in the richness of its colors and markings. It is abundant in most parts of California.

The California mountain quail, the largest and one of the handsomest of this group, inhabits the wooded mountains of the Pacific coast, and bears a superficial resemblance to the red-legged partridge of Europe. Like the Mearns quail, its haunts are usually more remote from cultivated lands than are those of the other species.

The services to agriculture of the western quails, while in most cases appreciable, are far less valuable than those of bobwhite, mainly because the birds are much less insectivorous. Moreover, the California valley quail sometimes damages the grape crop.

The value of a single game bird is of course small, and it is from this narrow point of view that its relation to the community is usually considered. When, however, the value of any important species is worked out the result is surprising. It has been conclusively demonstrated that in Virginia and North Carolina alone the common quail annually destroys many tons of noxious insects and weed seeds. The great value of this service must be apparent to all who appreciate the never-ending warfare between the farmer and his hydra-headed enemies, the insects and weeds. The food value also of the quail is great, and the health and pleasure derived from their pursuit has resulted in the investment of millions of dollars. When it is generally understood that by judicious effort the numbers of these useful birds may be greatly increased. with a proportionate benefit to all concerned, it is hoped that efforts to this end will not be long delayed.

THE BOBWHITE.

(Colinus virginianus.)[a]

The bobwhite is one of the most widely distributed and popular game birds of the United States, but in many places it is suffering ruthless extermination. Sportsmen, farmers, legislators, and ornithologists, as well as the friends of birds in general, should interest themselves in the problem of its preservation. In the Northern, Western, and Middle States it is commonly known as 'quail,' in the Southern States as 'partridge.' This tends to confusion, since in New England and northern New York the name 'partridge' is commonly applied to the ruffed grouse. Both names were brought to America by English colonists from their Old World homes, where they are applied to species not originally inhabiting this continent. The name 'bobwhite' is from the familiar call note of the bird.

In some of its characteristics bobwhite differs strikingly from other members of the family. For example, the crest—a well-developed adornment of several closely related American quails—in bobwhite is invisible except when the bird is excited.

The common bobwhite ranges more or less generally over the eastern half of the United States and southern Ontario, except in the colder, mountainous parts, from southern Maine to northern Florida, and west to South Dakota, Nebraska, Kansas, and Texas. In addi-

---

[a] The name is used here in its broad sense to cover the typical bird of the Eastern States, *Colinus virginianus*, and the two subspecies, the Florida bobwhite (*C. v. floridanus*) and the Texas bobwhite (*C. v. texanus*).

tion, colonies have been introduced and found to thrive in various localities in Colorado, New Mexico, Utah, Idaho, California, Oregon, Washington, and the island of Jamaica. South of the home of the typical bird, just outlined, bobwhites have a wide range, occupying Florida, western and southern Texas, Cuba, and a large part of Mexico, and extending even beyond the border of Guatemala. Owing chiefly to climatic influences the southern birds differ more or less from the northern ones. The masked bobwhite (*Colinus ridgwayi*), a closely related but separate species, once lived in extreme southern Arizona and the adjoining part of Sonora, but now it is probably extinct within our borders. With this exception all of the bobwhites from Canada to Guatemala and Cuba, according to E. W. Nelson, belong to a single species modified by environment into a considerable number of forms, some of which are strikingly different from the birds of the United States. The Florida bobwhite, which is peculiar to the peninsula of Florida, is smaller and darker than the northern bird. The Texas bobwhite of western Texas and northeastern Mexico is about the same size as the northern one, but is paler and has a light rufous collar below the black band and bordering the white throat patch. The Salvin bobwhite from the southern border of Mexico is very unlike the common bird of the United States, most of the head, neck, and breast being plain black and the rest of the underparts plain rufous.

The present account is limited to the bobwhites of the United States, including the Texas and Florida forms. The writer's field work in this connection has been principally in New Jersey, Virginia, and Maryland—on a farm at Marshall Hall, Md., which is directly across the Potomac from Mount Vernon.

CALL NOTES.

In the field the nuptial call note of the cockbird is an infallible guide to its identity. This familiar challenge, sounding to the sportsman like '*bob white*,' '*bob-bob-white*,' and to the farmer like '*more wet*' or '*no more wet*,' is by no means the only note of the species during the breeding season. It was the good fortune of the writer during the last week of June, 1902, to hear the nesting note and other calls. Again and again the cock left his distant perch, where he had been whistling 'bob white,' and, still calling, approached the nest on the bank of a little sluggish briery run between open fields. When within 50 yards of his mate he uttered the rally note, so thrilling to the sportsman in the fall, '*ka-loi-kee*,' which the hen often answered with a single clear whistle. Then followed a series of queer responsive 'caterwaulings,' more unbirdlike than those of the yellow-breasted chat, suggesting now the call of a cat to its kittens, now the scolding of a caged gray squirrel, now the alarm notes of a mother grouse blended with the strident cry of the guinea hen. As a finale sometimes came a loud rasping noise, not unlike the effort of a broken-voiced whip-poor-will. The favorite calling stations were rail fences at a height from 5 to 10 feet, and the limbs of trees along fence rows. One bird whistled in a tulip tree at least 35 feet from the ground. H. H. Miller reports that April 25, 1903, was the earliest date of nuptial notes at Sandy Spring, Md. After the breeding season the bird discontinues this characteristic call. During August 19–21, 1902, it was heard only on one occasion at Marshall Hall, where the birds are numerous, and ceased after a dozen repetitions. Edward A. Preble, of the Biological Survey, has recorded the 'bob-white' call at Wilmington, Mass., as late as October 20.

The notes of the bobwhite in fall and winter have been described by many writers. The following quotation from Mr. Sandys gives an admirable description of the call notes of a covey that has been scattered by the sportsman and is trying to reassemble for the night, a notation so accurate as instantly to recall the notes to one who has heard them: " Over the brow of a hill comes the low, tender call of the hen to her youngsters, ' *ka-loi-kee, ka-loi-kee;* ' and, perhaps, from the broomsedge beside the observer comes the loud vibrant answer, ' *whoil-kee.*' " This call is usually sounded in the late afternoon, but December 31, 1901, at Woodbridge, Va., a scattered flock was heard calling persistently in the morning.

On one occasion the writer watched a bobwhite whistling from a fence rail 10 feet away. At such close range the whistle lost all its melody and became a nasal shriek which was almost painful to the ear. It was repeated on an average five or six times a minute and consisted of either two or three notes, of which the first was so low as to be inaudible a hundred yards away, and the last was strikingly louder. The mode of delivery was peculiar; sitting in a normal, erect position the bird emitted the first note, then depressing the tip of the bill almost to touch its breast, with a motion as though hiccoughing, it gave the second, then throwing back its head and pointing its bill skyward it uttered the explosive, far-reaching third note.

BREEDING HABITS.

The nesting time of bobwhite in each section of the bird's range is usually limited to a fairly well-defined period, but varies considerably in the time of beginning, the difference being partly seasonal and partly regional. About Washington, D. C., the coveys usually break up the first part of May, one covey being seen in 1899 as late as May 9. In 1902 the first nest with eggs was found at Marshall Hall on May 29, and the first downy chicks on July 6. Between the end of June and last of August seven pairs of birds were found there which had recently mated or were incubating. This was shown by the fact that the cock birds were flushed thirty-six times and the hens only four times. During the same season five nests were found between July 15 and 19 at Sandy Spring, Md., less than 20 miles away. One of these nests contained 24 eggs. Even larger clutches are recorded, and one nest found at Woodstock, Ohio, is reported to have contained 42 eggs.[a] Such large clutches probably are the product of more than one bird. In 1903 nesting appeared to be later than in 1902, as the first eggs found were discovered July 10. The farmers at Marshall Hall say that they usually find the first downy chicks during wheat harvest, usually the last week of June. A number of broods of chicks were seen about Marshall Hall from July to September.

The newly hatched young have chocolate-streaked heads, and resemble small black and red bantam chicks. Whenever these newly hatched chicks remain motionless their protective coloration renders them invisible unless one makes a most careful search.

From information at hand it appears that the main breeding season for bobwhite in the Northern States, including the country about Washington, D. C., is during May, June, and the first half of July. Florida birds begin to breed regularly the first of April (though some are much earlier), and continue nesting till well into June. Texas birds nest mainly in April and May, but some nest as late as September. Throughout its range some of the birds breed earlier and others later than the main body of the species, and the occurrence of second or even third broods may lengthen the season. Robert Ridgway found a clutch of freshly deposited eggs in southern Illinois on October 16, and H. C. Munger found another set in Missouri in January, the parent being afterwards found frozen on the nest. Authentic records from various parts of its range show that bobwhite has been known to breed, at least occasionally, somewhere in its range every month of the year except December. This seems to prove that under certain circumstances bobwhite, like the domestic hen, will lay a clutch of eggs at any time of year.

The occasional presence with the female of young of two or three sizes appears to show that at least two broods are sometimes raised in a season, but we lack definite information on this subject. Major Bendire gives twenty-four days as the period of incubation. The male is reported as sometimes assisting in this duty.

<hr>

[a] Forest and Stream, X, p. 399, 1878.

GENERAL HABITS OF THE BOBWHITE.

The habits of bobwhite, like those of many other birds, vary considerably, and the following, observed by E. W. Nelson, is a case in point. In 1875 the Wabash bottoms near Mount Carmel, Ill., were covered with a magnificent forest, quite tropical in the size and luxuriant growth of trees and other vegetation. Scattered here and there through the forest were small clearings planted to corn. Bobwhites were found about all of these clearings, and the males were commonly heard calling from the tops of tall trees in the edge of the bordering forest, and on more than one occasion were stalked and shot in the midst of the woods from tree tops more than 100 feet from the ground. When flushed in the cornfields the coveys dashed away into the forest, where they took refuge in the tree tops, thence sending forth their rallying call notes.

There appears to be a tendency among bobwhites, at least in some regions, to a local migration. In certain sections, as in Virginia and Maryland, they commonly leave their summer homes on the approach of winter and congregate near the larger watercourses. In an old number of the American Sportsman Lewis refers to this fall movement, and says: "At this period the birds are said to be running or traveling, and will not lie to a dog; and to pursue is lost time, as it will be found utterly impossible to keep up with them, no matter with what speed you attempt it."

The habits of the bobwhite during the hunting season are well known. The birds move about most actively and feed in the early morning and late afternoon. The best shooting is to be had the hour before sunset, in the places where the birds have decided to spend the night. They roost on the ground, forming a solid ring with tails in and heads out. In Virginia and Maryland the roosting places are almost never in the woods, though in Mecklenburg County, Va., the writer has found them in grassy, briery little clearings among pine woods. At Marshall Hall the birds were found roosting in the edges of woodland, orchards, patches of ragweed in wheat stubble, cornfields, truck plats, broomsedge, dewberry and blackberry tangles, pastures, and fence corners. In Massachusetts Edward A. Preble found no roosts in the open fields, but found them among scrub oaks and in tall pine forests. Bobwhites habitually use a roosting ground again and again. A covey of a dozen, found the middle of November, 1899, at Marshall Hall, resorted to a corner of a peach orchard for eight consecutive nights, and during December, 1902, a covey of fifteen on the Roanoke River bottom used a narrow strip of cockleburr, ragweed, and smartweed for ten consecutive nights. It is interesting to note that, although quail seek the woods for shelter from enemies during the day, they generally regard the open as safer at night.

It is the general opinion that with the on-coming of winter the bobwhite is found less often in the open fields, where withered herbaceous plants afford but scant protection from enemies, than in dense bushy briery coverts and woods.

In Maryland and Virginia the scattered and depleted coveys after the shooting season evidently unite into large bevies. Their favorite resort in severe weather is a bank with southern exposure and suitable food supply. At Marshall Hall during one of the heaviest snowfalls of the season, when the Potomac was frozen over and the thermometer near zero, a covey was always to be found on the southeast side of a steep bank bordering a large swamp. Here the birds found food and warmth, for the rays of the sun fell on this slope so directly that even when the snow elsewhere lay from 3 to 6 inches deep it was here melted or remained only in patches. It was noticeable that when snow was on the ground the birds ventured only a few rods from cover, a fact that apparently indicated their appreciation of danger from the numerous hawks and foxes. At Kinsale, Va., the writer found bobwhites crossing open fields when there was an inch or two of snow, though for the most part they kept close to cover. In April and May the birds again venture out into the open, and they breed when vegetation is sufficiently grown to conceal the nests.

At Marshall Hall little oval pits in dry soil, in which quail had been dusting, were found in various situations, usually under cover of weeds and bushes about the fields. Dusting is a part of the toilet of all gallinaceous and many other birds, and may also be a protection against vermin.

BOBWHITE AS AN ALLY OF THE FARMER.

In summing up the relations of the bobwhite to agriculture it will be well to emphasize certain facts developed by our investigation of its food habits. In the first place, careful observations at Marshall Hall, where the acreage under cultivation is large and the bobwhite abundant, and less extended investigations elsewhere afford no evidence that the species does appreciable injury to crops of grain or fruit. Further, its habit of destroying weed seeds is of much economic importance. For instance, it is reasonable to assume that in the States of Virginia and North Carolina, from September 1 to April 30, the season when the largest proportion of weed seed is consumed by birds, there are four bobwhites to each square mile of land, or 354,820 in the two States. The crop of each bird holds half an ounce of seeds and is filled twice a day. Since at each of the two daily meals weed seeds constitute at least half the contents of the crop, or a quarter of an ounce, a half ounce daily is consumed by each bird. On this basis the total consumption of weed seeds by bobwhites from September 1 to April 30 in Virginia and North Carolina amounts to 1,341 tons. It is to be remembered also that if it were not for foxes, hawks, and trespassing pot hunters the birds would be more abundant and their services correspondingly greater. Insects form about one-third of the bobwhite's diet from June 1 to August 31; and a calculation similar to the one employed above shows that 340 tons of insects are destroyed during this period.

Among the insects consumed by the bird are such very harmful pests as the Rocky Mountain locust, the chinch bug, the Colorado potato beetle, the Mexican cotton boll weevil, cutworms, the two cotton worms, and the army worm. The highly insectivorous chicks cause a proportionally greater destruction of insects than the adult birds. Further, while many other useful birds confine themselves to the woodland or swamp, or merely scout along waterways, hedges, and fence rows, the bobwhite feeds directly among field crops. In the South it is found in cotton fields; in the North it delights in the ragweed-grown wheat stubble; in the West its favorite feeding ground is corn fields, and it often spends the night there instead of flying to cover as do most birds. The facility with which it passes from field to field, either on foot or on the wing, distributes its services to an unusual degree.

BOBWHITE AS AN ASSET OF THE FARM.

Every landowner should realize the value of the bobwhite, and should demand from sportsmen a fair price for the birds killed on his property. With proper management some farms of from 500 to 1,000 acres would probably yield a better revenue from bobwhites than from poultry. Many farms in North Carolina derive a regular income from this source. This is obtained by leasing the shooting right to wealthy sportsmen, who, in localities where birds are abundant, willingly pay considerable sums for the privilege. This is probably the most profitable use to which certain poor lands in the South can be put. In some places in Maryland, Virginia, and North Carolina the sportsman often pays the landowner from 5 to 25 cents for every bird shot. In other places the farmer or his boy is hired as guide to locate the quail. In addition the sportsman pays liberally for his board and otherwise adds to the farmer's income. Wide-awake farmers appreciate the fact that the genuine sportsman pays well for his sport and should discriminate between him and the market hunter. Millions of dollars can be realized by the proper management of the quail crop of the United States. The time is perhaps not far distant when landowners will protect their game birds from foxes, injurious hawks, and human poachers as diligently as they now do their poultry. The sooner the farmer realizes the value of the bobwhite and the fact that the market hunter is a bird exterminator, profiting at the landowner's expense, the better will be his chance of an income from his crop of quail.

BOBWHITE AS AN ARTICLE OF FOOD.

Perhaps no game is more generally known and liked than quail. The flesh of the bobwhite is juicy, tender, delicately flavored, easily digested, and nutritious. It is well adapted to the needs of invalids. To the farmer's table, where fresh meat is often not obtainable, this bird furnishes a welcome supply. No game is so much sought for in market, and countless numbers are sold every year. The writer knows of a single dealer in Washington who in 1902 sold 100,000 quail. Yet the supply is far short of the demand, and the price is constantly rising. In connection with the present price, which is $3 to $5 a dozen, it is interesting to recall Audubon's statement that in 1810 these birds could be bought for 12 cents a dozen and in 1831 for 50 cents.[a] Then they were on the tables of rich and poor alike.

BOBWHITE AS AN OBJECT OF SPORT.

Edwyn Sandys says of the bobwhite: "He truly is the king of his race; and not alone that, for, in the opinion of hosts of enthusiastic sportsmen, he is the best bird that flies." The well-known author T. S. Van Dyke says: " Dear little Bob White has brought more rest to the business-wearied soul, more new life to tired humanity than nearly all other American game combined." The pursuit of many kinds of game is possible only in the distant wilderness, where traveling is difficult and the exposure incident to the sport may be dangerous to health; but the pursuit of the bobwhite belongs to open, accessible country, and is not too severe for men accustomed to a sedentary life. To thousands of such men quail hunting is the yearly means of restoration, and results in a direct benefit to the community, though one not readily computed in money value. At a conservative estimate, between 300,000 and 400,000 sportsmen go out from cities every fall to hunt bobwhite, which means a large expenditure of money, much of which goes to farmers who hold shooting land. Such revenue is timely, for it comes when farm work yields small returns and employment is welcome. Where nonresident licenses are required, with fee of from $5 to $25, the State also derives a direct income from the sport.

The bobwhite deservedly stands at the head of American game birds, because it lies so well to the dog, and when flushed springs from the earth like an arrow, demanding a quick eye and a trained

---

[a] Ornith. Biog., I, p. 392, 1831.

touch on the trigger to bring it to bag. When, at the advance of the hunter, the covey explodes like a bomb, his skill is sharply tested if he would bring one of the whirring, meteorlike projectiles to the ground. Birds of a scattered covey are hard to find. Good authorities say that when they alight they remain quiet and compress their feathers to the body, with the result of withholding the scent. Many sportsmen, therefore, before hunting a scattered covey, give them time to run about and leave scent.

Paradoxical as it may seem, sportsmen exert a powerful influence for the protection of bobwhite. Many individuals and clubs own or lease large tracts, where they maintain the birds and shoot only the surplus. These enthusiasts assist in the enforcement of game laws, restock depleted covers, and provide food for the birds in times of scarcity. Certain clubs are organized for the purpose of holding field trials, the object of which is to test the ability of competing dogs to find and point birds. As retrieving is not required, the birds are not shot. One of the best-known patrons of field trials recently told the writer that he had not killed a bobwhite in ten years. A number of clubs control each a preserve of from 5,000 to 20,000 acres, on which no shooting is allowed—or, if permitted, is carefully regulated—and suitable measures are taken for protecting birds and facilitating their propagation. These trials are held in a score or more of States, and in some of the larger contests more than a hundred dogs are entered. Some owners of field-trial dogs have preserves of their own, stocked with hundreds of pairs of bobwhites. Thousands of live birds for the above purposes are in demand, at high prices. If the bobwhite could be domesticated and reared in captivity for sale, the enterprise would doubtless be very profitable. From these facts it is evident that the sport of hunting bobwhite contributes to the health and happiness of thousands of men, and that in various ways it can be made to add to the prosperity of farmers and others interested.

ESTHETIC VALUE OF BOBWHITE.

Much money has been spent, and well spent, merely for the enjoyment of the beauty and companionship of birds. For the protection of gulls and terns along the Atlantic coast thousands of dollars have been expended at the instance of bird lovers, in whose eyes these delicate and graceful creatures are the crowning attractions of marine landscape. In like manner the admirers of bobwhite derive esthetic pleasure from his presence. To pastoral inland scenes—woodlots in a green mist of young leaves, summer grass fields and bushy pastures, brown stubble, and skeleton cornfields—the bobwhite adds a distinctive charm—homely, but none the less attractive. As the bird calls from the fence post or runs fearlessly across the road, the stroller can but admire its trim, alert figure and tasteful color pattern of black, white, and brown, set off with delicate tintings of blue-gray. Its mellow whistle seems a proffer of good-fellowship, investing even a solitude with cheer, while the plaintive covey-call heard in the growing darkness to summon a scattered flock to the nightly resting place is one of the tenderest of evening sounds. Because of such traits the bird has made many friends, some of whom spend time and money to insure its undisturbed presence in their neighborhood.

DECREASE OF BOBWHITE.

Every few years, on the recurrence of unusually severe winters with heavy snows which cover the food supply, great numbers of bobwhites perish, and sometimes in the northern part of its range the bird becomes almost extinct. This unnecessary loss of life could be largely prevented if landowners and others interested would scatter a little grain in suitable places. This is done in some localities, as at Sandy Spring, Md., where H. H. Miller drives over the snow-covered country, scattering grain for the starving quail. The practice is worthy of general adoption. It is necessary only while the ground is snowbound, and especially after sleet storms.

The bobwhite has taken kindly to civilization and has followed the plow of the settler into new sections, so that with the advance of the farming area in the West, and especially in the Northwest, its range has been much extended.

There is little doubt, however, that, while the bobwhite is a fairly hardy and prolific species, its numbers are decreasing in much, if not all, of its range, where not specially protected. In the early fifties Lewis reported 61 birds killed in a day to a single muzzle loader, and mentions 900 birds trapped on one estate in a season. Within the last few years the scarcity of bobwhites has been so notable that several projected field trials have been abandoned for lack of birds on which to try the dogs.

Severe winters, as already noted, are an occasional cause for a great decrease in the number of the birds, though they increase rapidly with a few succeeding good seasons. In sections where the birds are still common unlimited slaughter is often indulged in by thoughtless hunters. Recent instances of such slaughter are on record, and the following may be cited: A bag of 175 birds to three guns in eight hours in the fall of 1902 at Tiffin, Ohio,[a] another of 300 birds to a single gun in a day and a half in the fall of 1902, in Marshall County, Ky.,[b] and still another of 292 birds to three guns in a day in South

---

[a] Recreation, vol. 17, p. 120.   [b] Ibid., vol. 19, p. 41.

Carolina during the same season.[a] The value of this bird, both to the farmer and the sportsman, renders the question of its maintenance and increase one of much importance. So assiduously is the bobwhite sought by sportsmen and market hunters that intelligent and concerted efforts are needed even to maintain its present numbers.

LEGISLATION IN BEHALF OF BOBWHITE.

In addition to natural causes, reasons for the diminished numbers of bobwhites are diversity in the open season, shooting out of season, excessive shooting in season, and unrestricted shooting and trapping for market. Lack of uniformity in laws of adjoining States, and in some cases of adjoining counties, renders their observance difficult and their enforcement often impossible. No other game bird has been the subject of so much legislation, which, beginning in New York in 1791, now extends to every State and Territory where the bird is native or has been introduced. The length of season during which the bird should be protected by law is a matter of paramount importance. It goes without saying that no shooting should be permitted during the breeding season, which must be understood to last until the young of the year are strong of wing and fully developed for the struggle for existence. Besides this the close season ought to include months of rest, during which the birds can fortify themselves for the physiological strain of the next period of reproduction. As now established the open season varies from twenty-one days in Ohio to seven months in Mississippi. In North Carolina, however, where nearly every county has its own law, the bobwhite may be shot throughout the year in five counties. Virginia has recently abolished county laws and established uniformity, an example that other States, especially Southern States, would do well to follow. It is gratifying to note that in 1903 the open seasons were shortened by New York, Illinois, Texas, and Virginia. In eight States—Maine, Rhode Island, Wisconsin, North Dakota, Montana, Colorado, Wyoming, and Utah—the bobwhite is absolutely protected for a term of years, extending to 1920 in Colorado. Two conditions justify such prohibition of shooting. First, when excessive shooting or other causes have made recuperation necessary; second, when birds just introduced into a new locality need time to establish themselves. Wherever the bird can not hold its own with an open season of three weeks absolute protection for a period of years is demanded. The length of the open season must vary with varying conditions, but in view of the general decrease of the birds there would seem to be a growing need for shortening it. The sooner Northern States limit their shooting to one month the better. Even

---

Southern birds can not stand the present continuous fusillade of from four to seven months, and the open season in the South should be limited to two or, at most, three months.

The slaughter of the bobwhite by sportsmen who hunt for pleasure is insignificant in comparison with that by professional market hunters. At the present time (1904), in about 25 States, the law takes cognizance of this fact by prohibiting the sale of birds killed within the State or imported from other States, and the general tendency altogether to prohibit the sale is growing each year. Every State except Mississippi forbids the sending of certain game outside the State—a restriction on the sportsman as well as the market hunter, although the privilege of carrying home a limited amount of game is often granted under a nonresident license. Fourteen States have laws, also affecting both classes, limiting a day's bag to from 5 to 50 birds. Many sportsmen and farmers would be glad if the limit were set at 12. Laws discriminating against nonresidents protect the game and benefit the landowner, provided visiting sportsmen are not barred altogether by unreasonable fees. Thirty-one States and Territories require nonresident licenses. In addition to State game laws there are certain Federal laws, the most important of which is the Lacey Act, which provides, among other things, through the Department of Agriculture, for the preservation, distribution, introduction, and restoration of game birds, and also undertakes to bring to justice persons who transport from one State to another game killed in violation of local laws. The latter clause proves effective in restricting such illegal shipments and in suppressing professional dealers that kill out of season in one State and attempt to sell in another where the season is still open. A law to prevent keeping birds in cold storage from one season to another would stop certain loopholes in the present laws and greatly aid in preserving game. An effective system of State game officials where it is lacking would aid in enforcing game laws. A number of States depend solely on county officers; but experience has shown that without a central State organization and special game wardens the law to a great extent becomes a dead letter.

MEASURES FOR PRESERVATION AND PROPAGATION.

Stringent laws against trapping the bobwhite have been enacted, but such legislation should permit legitimate trapping for purposes of propagation. One of the most important problems before game commissioners is the restocking of depleted covers. If, however, the bobwhite can be reared successfully in captivity, all trapping may be prohibited. The sporting magazines ('Forest and Stream' and 'American Field') mention cases of the bird's laying in captivity and raising its young; and in a letter to the writer, dated September 2, 1904, G. W. Jack, of Shreveport, La., says:

I now have a pair of quails (bobwhites) which were trapped last winter and which I keep in a large wire coop. They have made a nest in some grass and have laid about 12 or 15 eggs.

The eggs were laid very irregularly, not more than two or three a week, so that by the time the nest was full the season was far advanced, which perhaps accounts for the female not sitting. The eggs were set under a hen and proved fertile, but the young were eaten by the chicken as fast as they hatched. I concluded that this irregularity or slowness in laying was the result of the lack of insect and other egg-producing food, as the birds subsist almost wholly on grain. Of late, however, they have learned to eat with much relish the yolk of an egg hard boiled.

The failure of the female to sit was probably due to the unnatural confinement in so small a space, a difficulty which could readily be remedied if attempts to raise quail were made on a large scale. Unquestionably, too, it would be necessary to feed the quail, at least during the nesting period, to a considerable extent upon animal food.

An instructive account of quail breeding in confinement appears in Forest and Stream for September 28, 1882 (p. 164). The female had been hatched and reared by a bantam hen, and this circumstance has an important bearing on experiments of this kind. It is altogether probable that bobwhites hatched and reared in this way would lend themselves to experiments in propagation far more readily than wild birds trapped for the purpose.

The Department of Agriculture obtained three pairs of bobwhites from Kansas, which after five months' captivity are almost as wild as when first caged and show no signs of mating. Experiments in the domestication of bobwhite are well worth trying, however, because of the demand from clubs and individuals for live birds to restock their grounds. So great has become the demand in recent years that it is estimated that 200,000 birds would be required annually to fill it. During the spring of 1903 the demand far exceeded the supply, even at $5 a dozen, and sometimes at twice that figure.

Success in increasing the numbers of bobwhite depends largely on controlling its natural enemies, which include snakes, foxes, weasels, minks, skunks, domestic cats, and certain hawks and owls. Several species of snakes eat its eggs and young. Writing from Texas, Major Bendire says: "The many large rattlesnakes found here are their worst enemies. One killed in May had swallowed five of these birds at one meal; another had eaten a female, evidently caught on her nest, and half a dozen of her eggs; a third had taken four bobwhites and a scaled partridge."[a] In Mecklenburg County, Va., the

---

[a] Life Hist. N. Am. Birds [1], p. 8, 1892.

king snake (*Lampropeltis getula*) has been known to eat a clutch of eggs. At Falls Church, Va., Harvey Riley captured a black snake (*Bascanion constrictor*) which disgorged a newly hatched bobwhite. Reference has been made already to the marked decrease in the number of bobwhites on the 230-acre farm at Marshall Hall, from fifty-odd birds in July to less than a dozen in December, though not more than a dozen had been shot. This decrease was probably due, at least in part, to gray foxes; for in August and September these animals were numerous, and often came after the chickens within a stone's throw of the farmhouse. Other predaceous mammals and birds of prey were not numerous, but foxes frequently were seen at midday searching through pastures where there were broods of bobwhites. It must be easy for a fox to exterminate a whole brood of newly hatched bobwhites, and no difficult task to catch them even when three-fourths grown. Minks and weasels, when numerous, are probably even more destructive to young bobwhites than to domestic poultry. The domestic cat that takes to foraging in woods and fields is also a menace and should be shot on suspicion, for it undoubtedly preys on game birds, as it is known to do on song birds and young rabbits.

In Maryland and Virginia the writer has found the crow plundering nests of the bobwhite, and in these States the crow is an enemy also of poultry. Doctor Fisher states in his Hawks and Owls of the United States that of the forty-odd species which he studied he found only nine that killed the bobwhite. Four of these—the goshawk, Cooper hawk, sharp-shinned hawk, and great-horned owl—are very destructive to poultry as well as game. Dr. W. C. Strode, of Bernadotte, Ill., writes that bobwhite's worst enemy is the Cooper hawk. "A few days ago one flew up from the roadside when I was passing, and a bobwhite was dangling from one foot." During November, 1900, this species so persecuted the birds at Marshall Hall that they were seldom found far from cover. In one instance a hawk was seen to swoop to the ground and rise with a cock bobwhite. The other species of hawks and owls rarely molest quail.

If bobwhites more frequently nested along fence rows instead of in open mowing land, they would abound in many places where they are rare. The mowing machine lays many nests bare, and they are either despoiled by enemies or deserted by the old birds. At Sandy Spring, Md., early in July, 1903, four nests with their eggs were cut over in a 50-acre grass lot. In other hay fields several nests were discovered in time to leave grass uncut about them, but boys robbed them all. Between such lads and the crows and other enemies bobwhites have a hard time in certain sections.

To enable them to withstand the winter, bobwhites need suitable food and cover. In severe winters coveys are sometimes saved by being trapped and fed in confinement until spring. Naturally the birds suffer most in the northern part of their range, but there are reports of their death from severe and protracted cold in Maryland and Virginia. Sandys says: "The birds know when the snow is coming, and they creep under the brush, intending to remain there until the weather has cleared. * * * Then the rain comes and wets the surface all about, then the sleet stiffens it, * * * the cold becomes intense, and every foot of damp snow promptly hardens into solid ice. * * * The quail are now imprisoned beneath a dome of crystal, which may endure for days." [a] H. C. Oberholser says that in severe winters in Wayne County, Ohio, whole coveys are found dead from this cause. Dr. P. L. Hatch reports that in Minnesota the birds increase in numbers during years with mild winters and decrease when the winter is exceptionally severe.[b] Wilson Flagg states in Birds and Seasons of New England that thousands of bobwhites were destroyed by the deep snows of 1856–57. During the very severe winter of 1903–4 bobwhites were nearly exterminated in portions of Massachusetts. That quail do not always succumb to exceptional cold appears from the fact that in Susquehanna County, Pa., at an altitude of 2,000 feet, W. W. Cooke found a covey of a dozen bobwhites apparently in the best of condition on December 9, 1902, though a foot of snow covered the ground and the thermometer stood at 20° below zero.

A study of the winter habits of the bobwhite by the writer in the vicinity of Washington, D. C., so far has yielded only fragmentary results. In February, 1900, after a foot of snow had fallen, in a careful two days' search he failed to discover even a track of a large covey that usually frequented river flats along the Potomac at Marshall Hall. The birds must have been under the snow or back in the timber. At Falls Church, Va., after a lighter fall of snow he saw a covey of five moving among briers on the edge of a wood, and their fresh tracks showed that they had been feeding systematically on rose hips, but had not ventured from cover. At Cabin John Bridge, Md., after a snowfall of several inches his dog pointed six birds on the south side of a river bluff, where the sun had melted holes in the snow. On one of these bare spots he saw two birds, which rose and were joined by four others. The covey had made wallows 2 inches deep in the leaf mold on the bare spots. All the birds had avoided stepping on the snow. At hand was such food as the berries of sumac and the seeds of *Galactia volubilis* and *Chamæchrista fascicularis*. Examination of the droppings indicated that less than

---

[a] Upland Game Birds, p. 70, 1902.
[b] Notes on the Birds of Minnesota, p. 155, 1892.

one-tenth of the food had been animal matter, the remains of which consisted of ants, the tibiæ of grasshoppers, the spotted cuticle of soldier bugs, and the cow-horn-like mandibles of spiders. So far as could be made out, the remains of vegetable food consisted of the skin of kernels of corn, fragments of the akenes of ragweed, and pulverized bits of sumac seeds (*Rhus copallina*), partridge pea (*Chamæchrista fascicularis*), milk pea (*Galactia volubilis*), and crownbeard (*Verbesina*), besides unidentified leaf material. The weather had been severe for more than a week, but the birds were in good condition.

On the Marshall Hall farm, a short distance back from the banks of the Potomac, is a swamp that has a steep bank with a southern exposure where there is usually more or less bare ground in patches. For several years bobwhites have made a winter haunt of this warm, sunny bank, and here some interesting observations were made February 18 and 19, 1902, when the snow was from 2 to 4 inches deep and the minimum temperature was 4° F. above zero. A covey had spent the night of February 17 not on the warm bank, comparatively bare of snow, but on the level above the bank, where they had squatted on the snow under a dewberry bush among broomsedge. Their feet and droppings had melted the snow, and subsequent freezing had formed an icy ring. The birds had not flown thither, but had walked from the swamp up the steep bank and through the broomsedge level. The next morning they had flown from the roost to the steep slope, had run along the edge of the swamp to a bushy, tree-bordered stream, then up its north bank for 300 yards and back on the south bank, and thence to the steep, sunny slope again. On their journey they had gone under every matted tangle of cat-brier vines—possibly for berries, but more probably for protection. At one point they had fed freely on sumac berries. The tracks of a fox were found with those of the birds for about 100 yards. On the morning of the 19th they traveled not more than 200 yards, this chiefly among outstanding willows and alders of the swamp and along the belt of land 5 to 20 yards wide between the boundary fence and the reeds of the swamp. In one place two pairs of birds had walked so near together as to cross one another's tracks; two single birds had made clear lines of tracks on one side of them, and a single bird had walked alone on the other side from 1 to 4 feet from his nearest companion. All had evidently eaten rose hips, mutilated remains of which still clung to the bushes. The covey might have been expected to range far and wide in the open fields for seeds and even to straw ricks for grain, but except when traveling to their roost they had never gone more than a rod from cover. Apparently fear of enemies restrained them.

An article in the American Field, February 25, 1899, by the well-known sportsman John Bolus, of Wooster, Ohio, illustrates the hardiness of the bobwhite. When several inches of snow were on the ground and the thermometer registered from 15 to 27 degrees below zero every night for a week, Mr. Bolus took a tramp to see how the birds had fared. He found no dead birds, but saw six thrifty coveys—81 birds in all. They were feeding on ragweed projecting from the snow, and were jumping up to reach seeds on sprays above their heads. Some coveys remained under shelter of little weed patches, but others ranged over the more open fields.

In Maryland and Virginia large landowners often feed their birds in severe weather. Wheat and corn are the best food, and should be scattered, if possible, among the briers where the birds are safe from hawks. Bobwhites have been known to feed with chickens in barnyards. By a little forethought landowners and sportsmen can easily make winter provision for their birds. Sumac bushes should be left along hedgerows and the edge of woodland to furnish food that is always above the snow and lasts well into spring. Twelve bobwhites collected in December in North Dakota had made ninetenths of their food of sumac, having eaten from 50 to 300 berries each. A similar use, in coast regions, of the bayberry and wax myrtle has been noted. Their berries, as well as those of sumac, last till May, and the plants should always be spared by everyone who is interested in the welfare of the bobwhite. Smilax, affording little food but fine cover, and wild roses, giving both food and cover, are also valuable. Blackberry thickets, young pine woods, laurel, and holly furnish safe retreats from enemies.

The farmer can well afford to feed the bobwhite in winter, but he can not afford to spend as much time and money as the owner of game preserves, and for the latter class further suggestions may be helpful. In the Eastern and Southern States land that will not grow profitable crops may be used for the game preserve, provided it has water and bushy coverts. The use of the mowing machine, so destructive to eggs and young birds, should be avoided when possible during the breeding season. Wheat for the birds should be sown in long strips not over 50 yards wide. The best of the grain may be harvested and the rest left standing. On the stubble a luxuriant growth of ragweed will generally spring up—a perfect food supply, except that it does not last till spring; hence the need of sumac or bayberry. In regions too dry for ragweed to grow in the stubble, sunflowers are an excellent substitute. Sorghum, millet (*Chætochloa*), and possibly panicum may be planted and left standing. Pop corn will be found particularly valuable, as large corn can not easily be swallowed by the younger birds. Buckwheat, and in the South the nutritious cowpea, and the climbing false buckwheat, the thick tangles of which also afford good cover, bear excellent food. Other plants of the genus

Polygonum are fond of moist land, and furnish palatable seeds for the bobwhite; for instance, black bindweed (*Polygonum convolvulus*), Pennsylvania persicaria (*Persicaria pennsylvanicum*), and black heart (*Persicaria lapathifolia*). All wild leguminous plants should be left undisturbed, for the birds feed on seeds of most of our legumes. Small clumps of locusts may well be left in open fields to give both food and cover. Tick trefoil, bush clover, Japan clover, the milkpea, and the wild bean—all wild plants—are suitable for food. Of the summer fruits the dewberry is the most important, and in the absence of water furnishes a substitute; therefore these vines, nearly everywhere plentiful, should be left in places remote from water. A water supply is of course important. Streams with bush-grown banks through open fields are most valuable. Beside them will be found spreading panicum (*Panicum proliferum*), which shells out its grain a kernel or two at a time until well into spring. Birds find food, shade, water, and shelter in the vegetation along small streams. Marshes also afford cover and food. If connected with estuaries they often support a rank growth of wild rice, an ideal provision for birds. Sufficient shelter to protect the birds from hawks is almost indispensable. Oak and beech woods supply mast as well as shelter, but pines afford the best cover, and some of them, notably the longleaf pine, furnish food. A comfortable retreat for the coldest weather is invaluable. In Maryland and Virginia fields of heavy broomsedge answer this purpose well, but best of all is a steep bank with southern exposure, where the sun quickly melts the snow, and gives the birds a chance to forage on bare spots for food and gravel. If such a bank is not far from cover, and has a growth of briers on it to give the birds a feeling of security, it will become a favorite winter haunt and during severe weather is the best place to scatter grain. With a little help from man the bobwhite will be found to winter well even in the northern part of its range.

Bobwhite is prolific. A pair of birds under favorable conditions will raise a dozen young in a season. Then, too, it is long lived, for a bird kept in captivity is known to have reached the age of 9 years.[a] The outlook for the future of the species is most satisfactory, provided it is given even a small amount of care, with proper legal protection. The Audubon societies, with a membership of 65,000 to 70,000, which cherish the bobwhite for esthetic and humanitarian reasons, the sportsman who loves the whirr of its brown wings, and the farmer, whose enemies it destroys and whose resources it increases, can do much to favor the bird in its natural environment and to protect it by adequate and effectively enforced laws.

---

[a] Forest and Stream, VII, p. 407, 1876.

FOOD HABITS OF BOBWHITE.

Both field and laboratory investigations of the food habits of the bobwhite have been conducted by the Biological Survey. The field work was confined chiefly to Maryland and Virginia, and, although it represents in some degree every month in the year, has been limited mainly to the breeding and the hunting seasons. The laboratory work to determine the different kinds of food and their proportions has included examination of the contents of crops and gizzards from 918 birds. This material was collected from 21 States, Canada, the District of Columbia, and Mexico, but chiefly from New York, Maryland, Virginia, Florida, Illinois, South Dakota, Nebraska, Kansas, and Texas. Stomachs were obtained each month of the year, but unfortunately few were collected in the breeding season. Laboratory work included also feeding experiments with three pairs of captive bobwhites obtained from Kansas.

The bird's digestive organs are well adapted to the character of its diet. The stomach, or gizzard, as it is commonly called, is provided with powerful muscles for grinding the hard seeds on which the bird largely subsists. The crop, a sac like enlargement of the œsophagus, is a mere membranous receptacle for first receiving the food, and is without muscles. Its capacity is usually from four to six times that of the stomach.

The bobwhite is insectivorous as well as graminivorous. It is, in fact, one of our most nearly omnivorous species. In addition to seeds, fruit, leaves, buds, tubers, and insects, it has been known to eat spiders, myriapods, crustaceans, mollusks, and even batrachians. The food for the year as a whole, calculated by volume and determined by analysis of the contents of 918 stomachs, consisted of vegetable matter, 83.59 per cent, and animal matter, 16.41 per cent. In addition, there was mineral matter varying in amount from 1 to 5 per cent of the gross contents of the stomachs, and in exceptional cases rising to 30 per cent. This usually consisted of sand, with coarser bits of quartz 2 to 7 mm. in diameter, which were taken to pulverize the food and thus render it easier of assimilation.

The vegetable part of the food consisted of grain, 17.38 per cent; various seeds, chiefly weeds, 52.83 per cent; fruit, 9.57 per cent, and miscellaneous vegetable matter, 3.81 per cent. The animal matter in the food was distributed as follows: Beetles, 6.92 per cent; grasshoppers, 3.71 per cent; bugs, 2.77 per cent; caterpillars, 0.95 per cent; miscellaneous insects, 0.70 per cent; and other invertebrates, largely spiders, 1.36 per cent.

The insect food of bobwhite, in comparison with that of other birds, is interesting. It includes fewer caterpillars, ants, and other Hymenoptera, but more bugs; and, singularly enough in a terrestrial feeder, nearly twice as large a proportion of beetles as of grasshoppers. The meadow lark, per contra, another terrestrial feeder, takes 29 per cent of grasshoppers and only 18 per cent of beetles.

The food of the bobwhite for the year is noteworthy in several respects. Its character varies with the season. From October to March it consists almost exclusively of vegetable matter—for February and March 99.8 per cent of vegetable food appearing in analysis—while in late spring and in summer it is made up largely of insects, August showing 44.1 per cent of insect food. The grain taken, as a rule, is derived neither from newly sown fields nor from standing crops, but is gleaned from stubble fields after harvest. Grain forms a less prominent part of the food than the seeds of weeds, which are the most important element of all and make up one-half of the food for the year. The most distinctive feature of this, as a whole, is the large proportion—15.52 per cent—of leguminous seeds, a food seldom eaten by the various species of sparrows or other terrestrial feeders. A small fraction of this seed comes from cultivated plants, especially the cowpea; the rest is derived from wild plants, most of them classed as weeds. Leguminous seeds appear to be most largely consumed during December, when they form 25 per cent of the food. The 15.05 per cent of insect food, although a comparatively small part of the total, is of extreme importance, since it contains many pests that are generally avoided by nongallinaceous birds. Noteworthy among these are the potato beetle, twelve-spotted cucumber beetle, striped cucumber beetle, squash ladybird beetle, various cutworms, the tobacco worm, army worm, cotton worm, cotton bollworm, the clover weevil, cotton boll weevil, imbricated snout beetle, May beetle, click beetle, the red-legged grasshopper, Rocky Mountain locust, and chinch bug.

It should be observed that in the search for these pests and for weed seeds the bobwhite, unlike many birds of the woodland, hedgerow, and orchard, extends its foraging to the center of the largest fields, thus protecting the growing crops.

GRAIN AS FOOD.

Vegetable matter has long been known to be an important element of the food of the bobwhite; indeed, many people suppose that it constitutes the entire food of the bird. The impression that the bobwhite eats little else than grain has prevailed even among many sportsmen who have bagged most of their game in the stubble field. The present analysis, however, discloses that grain forms scarcely more than one-sixth of the food. Laboratory study shows that it is eaten in every month of the year, the maximum amount, 46 per cent of the food for the month, having been taken in March. In the specimens examined corn amounts to 11.96 per cent of the total food for the year, while all other kinds of grain collectively amount to only 5.42 per cent. Wheat (4.17 per cent) is next to corn in importance. As experiments with captive birds failed to show marked preference for either corn or wheat, the disproportion between the two above noted is probably due to the fact that more corn than wheat is grown in the country where our birds were obtained. The remaining cereal food (1.25 per cent of the total) is miscellaneous grain, including Kafir corn, sorghum, millet, buckwheat, barley, oats, and rye.

Grain-eating birds are likely to do much harm to crops. They may pull up sprouting grain, plunder the standing crop when it is in the milk, or forage among the sheaves at harvest time. The bobwhite, however, is a notable exception. The period of germination is the time when grain is liable to serious injury by birds. But not a single sprouting kernel was found in the crops and stomachs of quails examined. Field observations, during the years 1899 and 1900, at Marshall Hall gave similar evidence. While crows injured sprouting corn so seriously during May that several extensive replantings were necessary, bobwhites, unusually abundant in the vicinity at the same time, were never seen to disturb the germinating grain. During November, 1899, sprouting wheat was saved from crow blackbirds only by diligent use of the shotgun; but both then and in other seasons the bobwhite was rarely observed in winter-wheat fields and never was seen to molest the crop. Sprouting oats apparently were not molested, though extended observations were not made. No data are available for rye and millet, but in newly sown buckwheat fields in Essex County, N. J., which the writer saw ravaged by doves, there was no sign of injury by the bobwhites. Publications on economic ornithology and reports received by the Biological Survey add testimony of like character. It may safely be stated, therefore, that so far as at present known the bobwhite does no appreciable harm to sprouting grain.

In order to learn to what extent the species injures ripening grain, observations were made for several years at Marshall Hall. Unlike the crow and several kinds of blackbirds, the bobwhite did no damage there to corn in the milk, nor did it injure ripening wheat and oats. Flocks of English sparrows, however, might be seen feeding on wheat in the milk, and not uncommonly a score of goldfinches swayed on the panicles of ripening oats. A hen bobwhite shot in a field of ripe wheat, June 18, 1903, had much of the grain in its crop, though whether obtained from standing heads or from fallen kernels did not appear. As the bobwhite usually feeds on the ground, and as it was never seen feeding from the stalk at Marshall Hall, it appears probable that it seeks only the fallen grain. At wheat harvest it follows the binder, and at Marshall Hall was often seen in the harvest field picking up scattered wheat. It was not observed there on the shocks, appearing to find an abundance of waste kernels. At corn harvest also bobwhite takes its share from exposed ears; but the bird is not able to shuck corn, as do the crow and the wild goose. Several crops of ripe oats at Marshall Hall were watched during harvest time and furnished no evidence against the bobwhite. No report of injury by it elsewhere at harvest time has come to the Biological Survey, though damage may be done where peculiar local conditions conjoin with an overabundance of birds.

The bobwhite, however, is a persistent stubble feeder. As Mr. Sandys puts it, " He is the gleaner who never reaps, who guards the growing crops, who glories over a bounteous yield, yet is content to watch and wait for those lost grains which fall to him by right." Where fields of wheat stubble support a rank growth of ragweed the sportsman is most likely to find a feeding covey. At Marshall Hall, during September, October, and November, such fields are the favorite haunts of the birds. On this farm corn has a greater acreage than wheat, but the birds are much less often found in corn stubble; and, as stomach examinations show, they eat much less corn than wheat. Since experiments with captive birds showed no preference for wheat, food other than grain may have kept them on the wheat stubble. Along the Roanoke in Virginia, where wheat is not grown, bobwhites feed in corn fields.

On the Western prairies, where cornstalks left standing in the fields afford good cover, the birds are more often found in cornfields. Six birds collected from such fields in November, 1891, at Badger, Nebr., contained 181 whole kernels of corn; the smallest number in a crop was 20 and the largest 48.

It is not unusual to find from 100 to 200 grains of wheat in a crop. A bobwhite shot at West Appomattox, Va., in December, 1902, had its crop distended almost to bursting with 508 grains of wheat. This habit of gleaning waste grain after harvest is beneficial to the farm, for volunteer grain is not desirable, especially where certain insect pests or parasitic fungi are to be combated. As the scattered kernels are often too far afield to be gathered by domestic poultry, the services of the bobwhite in this respect are especially useful.

The bobwhite sometimes eats the seeds of certain cultivated leguminous plants. Both the black-eye and the clay cowpeas (*Vigna sinensis*) have been found in stomachs, and one contained 35 peas of the latter variety. In Westmoreland and Mecklenburg counties, Va., cowpea patches are favorite resorts for the birds in November and December. Garden peas were found in crops collected by Mr. Walter Hoxie at Frogmore, S. C. In rare instances the bobwhite picks up clover seeds, and it has been known to eat a lima bean. It may take also Kafir corn and sorghum, and it has a decided liking for millet (*Chætochloa italica*), a taste particularly noticeable in birds of Kansas, Nebraska, and South Dakota. A crop from Onaga, Kans., contained 1,000 millet seeds. No significant damage to millet has been reported and the birds may secure most of this food from stubble fields.

WEED SEEDS AS FOOD.

Weeds appropriate the space, light, water, and food of the plants that directly or indirectly support man. A million weeds may spring up on a single acre, and a single plant of one of these species may mature 100,000 seeds in a season. This process, if unchecked, may produce in the spring of the third year 10,000,000,000 weeds. The problem of weed destruction is perennial in every land; indeed, soil culture may be called a never ceasing war against weeds. Of the birds that aid the farmer in this struggle the bobwhite, the native sparrows, and the mourning dove are the most efficient. They attack weeds at that vital stage—the seed period—hence their work, especially against the annuals which depend on seeds for perpetuation, is of enormous practical value.

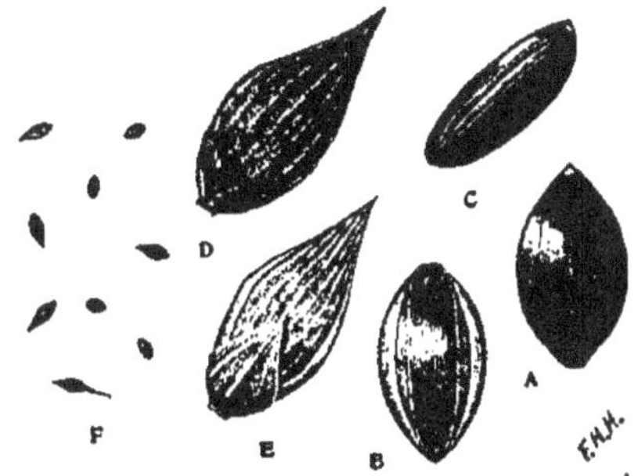

FIG. 1.—Seed of witch grass (*Panicum capillare*). (From Bull. 38, Nevada Agricultural Experiment Station.)

The bobwhite is preeminently a seed eater, 52.83 per cent of its food for the year consisting of seeds. The bulk of these are the seeds of plants belonging to the general category of weeds. Many of them are injurious plants with which the farmer is constantly at strife; others are less noxious and some are seldom, if ever, troublesome. Sixty-odd species are known to be eaten, and thorough observations would probably raise the number to a hundred or more. The food of no other bird with which the writer is acquainted is so varied. At Marshall Hall and in Mecklenburg and Westmoreland counties, Va., a somewhat detailed study was made of the weed seed eaten by the bird. At Marshall Hall fields of wheat stubble grown up to ragweed were favorite feeding grounds. Among others found there were buttonweed seeds, each like a miniature horsehoof, complete even to the frog; 20 or 30 of these were sometimes contained in a single stomach. A number of birds shot on wheat stubble had eaten largely of bastard pennyroyal seeds, which are rough and resemble blackberry seeds. Goldfinches and other seed eaters also find these palatable. Along ditches the abundant grasses—witch grass (fig. 1) and spreading panicum—provide the birds with shade in summer and a continuous harvest through the winter. The grain, inclosed in a cylindrical sheath which opens at the top, is rattled out, a few kernels at a time, by the strong fall and winter winds. Along the same ditches, especially in damper places among trees and bushes, another plant, the jewel weed, flourishes. Its ripened seeds, hurled from the opening pods by elastic coiled springlike valves, are eaten in large numbers by the bobwhite. The jewel-weed cotyledons are inclosed in a plain seed coat; but the cotyledons themselves are of a delicate robin's-egg blue, rounded and colored like tiny turquoises.

Several weeds injurious to truck crops are useful to the bobwhite. In a field where crab grass as a thick mat had overrun a patch of yams a covey spent much time gathering the seeds (fig. 2). In

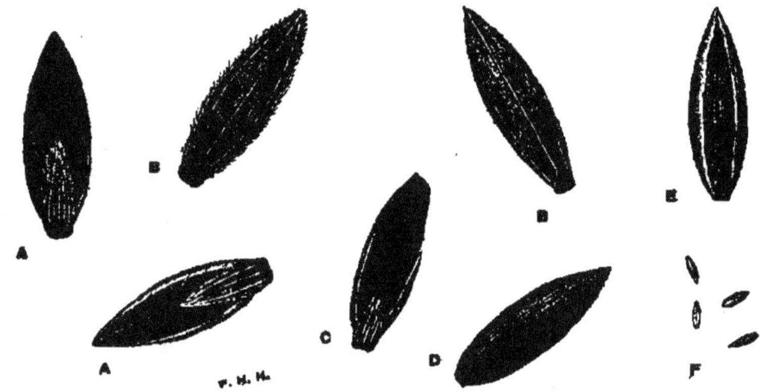

Fig. 2.—Seed of crab grass (*Syntherisma sanguinalis*). (From Bull. 47. Nevada Agricultural Experiment Station.)

another place where lamb's-quarters was 6 feet high and pigweed still higher, a flock of busy weeders could almost always be flushed at certain hours. Patches of green foxtail grass often attracted a covey for an evening feed. In the northern part of the United States this plant grows rank, and in many sections furnishes the bird its main food for September and October. Near a stream in a truck flat was a forest of giant ragweed from 8 to 10 feet high, and here bobwhites were frequently seen picking up scattered seeds. Their favorite weed seed, however, is the common, or smaller, rag-weed. At Marshall Hall this weed springs up, not only on truck land, but most luxuriantly in wheat stubble after harvest, covering the field with a rank growth 3 feet high. When abundant, its seeds are eaten in the fall more than those of any other plant, supplying a little over 16 per cent of the total food during October, November, and January. The fruits beset with a crowning circlet of spines are taken into the crop whole. In the stomach the brown oval seeds are freed from the spiny outer coat, crushed by the powerful muscular action, and made to yield their rich oily meat to the digestive juices.

In Mecklenburg County, Va., during the last week of December, 1902, a covey of a dozen bobwhites resorted to a cornfield to feed on the shining black seeds of smartweed, often a troublesome plant on low ground. In Westmoreland County, November, 1901, bobwhites fed freely on seeds of climbing false buckwheat, which festooned all the shrubbery along streams and afforded the birds admirable cover as well as food. The seeds of knot grass (fig. 3), a species related to the smartweeds and false buckwheat, also contribute to the food of the bobwhite.

The fondness of bobwhites for leguminous seeds has already been mentioned. On the edge of woodlands, along hedgerows, and to some extent in open ground, they consume large quantities of seeds of tick-trefoil, Japan clover, and bush clover, and their crops have been found distended with these seeds. They also find the partridge pea massed in great patches at Marshall Hall and in some places in Virginia, but it appears

FIG. 3.—Seed of knot grass (*Polygonum aviculare*). (From Bull. 88, Nevada Agricultural Experiment Station.)

to be of less importance to them. A few stomachs contained as many as 100 of these seeds. In several sections the butterfly pea was eaten in about the same proportion as the partridge pea. The hog peanut, like the butterfly pea, a trailing plant bearing a small grayish-brown bean, furnished several times as much food as the partridge pea and butterfly pea combined. Of these seeds 600 are sometimes eaten at a meal. Southern birds relish the Florida coffee seeds and lupine seeds. Seeds from locust pods also are frequently eaten by the bobwhite.

In the northeastern part of its range the bobwhite has been reported as feeding on seeds of the ill-scented skunk cabbage. Four of eight birds shot in October, 1902, at Wilmington, Mass., by Edward A. Preble, of the Biological Survey, had eaten them. These seeds are somewhat flattened and subspherical, and average about three-eighths of an inch in diameter. Two crops were filled with them, one containing 10 of these great seeds. This plant, abundant in northern swamps, may furnish food for birds in game preserves.

Seeds of different species of violets are often eaten. In some cases the three-valved seed pods, each valve containing a dozen or more seeds, had been swallowed entire. Seeds make up 50.36 per cent of the bobwhite's food, and a quantitative study of it shows that the grass family contributes 9.46 per cent; leguminous plants, 15.52 per cent; smartweed and other polygonums, 4.41 per cent; ragweed, 7.28 per cent; and miscellaneous weeds, 13.69 per cent. The number of seeds eaten at a meal may suggest the value of the bird as a weed destroyer. As many as 200 to 300 smartweed seeds, 500 seeds of red sorrel, and 700 seeds of three-seeded mercury have been taken at a meal. Crops and stomachs crammed with nothing but ragweed seeds are often found. A bird shot November 6, 1902, at Marshall Hall, had eaten 1,000 ragweed akenes; another killed there the previous November had eaten as many seeds of crab grass. Birds shot in Mecklenburg County, Va., contained about 2,000 leguminous seeds, mainly tick-trefoil, and various kinds of bush clover. A bird shot in October, 1902, at Pine Brook, N. J., had eaten 5,000 seeds of green foxtail grass, and one killed on Christmas day, 1901, at Kinsale, Va., had taken about 10,000 pigweed seeds.

LIST OF WEED SEEDS EATEN.

The list of seeds eaten, excluding mast and pine seeds, is as follows:

Slender paspalum (*Paspalum setaceum*).

Slender finger grass (*Syntherisma filiformis*).

Crab grass (*Syntherisma sanguinalis*).

Barnyard grass (*Echinochloa crusgalli*).

Barbed panicum (*Panicum barbulatum*).

Switch grass, tall smooth panicum (*Panicum virgatum*).

Spreading panicum (*Panicum proliferum*).

Witch grass (*Panicum capillare*).

Yellow foxtail (*Chætochloa glauca*).

Green foxtail (*Chætochloa viridis*).

Timothy (*Phleum pratense*).

Sheathed rush grass (*Sporobolus vaginæflorus*).

Slender spike grass (*Uniola laxa*).

Wild rice (*Zizania aquatica*).

Nut grass (*Cyperus rotundus*).

Rush (*Scirpus?*).

Sedge (*Carex* sp.).

Tussock sedge (*Carex stricta*).

Skunk cabbage (*Spathyema fœtida*).

Red sorrel (*Rumex acetosella*).

Curled dock (*Rumex crispus*).

Pale persicaria (*Persicaria lopathifolia*).

Pennsylvania persicaria (*Persicaria pennsylvanica*).

Smartweed (*Persicaria hydropiper*).

Knotweed (*Polygonum aviculare*).

Black bindweed (*Polygonum convolvulus*).

Climbing false buckwheat (*Tiniaria scandens*).

Lamb's-quarters (*Chenopodium album*).

Rough pigweed (*Amaranthus retroflexus*).

Carpet weed (*Mollugo verticillata*).

Corn cockle (*Agrostemma githago*).

Chickweed (*Alsine media*).

Charlock (*Raphanus raphanistrum*).

Witch hazel (*Hamamelis virginiana*).

Acacia (*Acacia* sp.).

Redbud (*Cercis canadensis*).

Sensitive pea (*Chamæcrista nictitans*).

Partridge pea (*Chamæcrista fascicularis*).

Cassia (*Cassia* sp.).

Lupine (*Lupinus* sp.).

Clover (*Trifolium* sp.).

Trefoil (*Lotus* sp.).

Psoralea (*Psoralea* sp.).

Locust (*Robinia pseudacacia*).

Florida coffee (*Sesban macrocarpa*).

Tick-trefoil (*Meibomia nudiflora* and *M. grandiflora*).

Hairy bush clover (*Lespedeza hirta*).

Creeping bush clover (*Lespedeza repens*).

Bush clover (*Lespedeza violacea*).

Japan clover (*Lespedeza striata*).

Vetch (*Vicia* sp.).

Hog peanut (*Falcata comosa*).

Downy milkpea (*Galactia volubilis*).
Prairie rhynchosia (*Dolicholus latifolius*).
Trailing wild bean (*Strophostyles helvcola*).
Pink wild bean (*Strophostyles umbellata*).
Crane's bill (*Geranium carolinianum*).
Yellow sorrel (*Oxalis stricta*).
Croton (*Croton* sp.).
Texas croton (*Croton texensis*).
Three-seeded mercury (*Acalypha gracilens*).
Spotted spurge (*Euphorbia maculata*).
Flowering spurge (*Euphorbia corollata*).
Red maple (*Acer rubrum*).
Box elder (*Rulac negundo*).
Jewel weed (*Impatiens* sp.).
Sida (*Sida spinosa*).
Violet (*Viola* sp.).
Ash (*Fraxinus* sp.).
Morning glory (*Ipomœa* sp.).
Bindweed (*Convolvulus* sp.).
Corn gromwell (*Lithospermum arvense*).
Hoary puccoon (*Lithospermum canescens*).
Gromwell (*Lithospermum officinale*).
Vervain (*Verbena stricta*).
Bastard pennyroyal (*Trichostema dichotomum*).
Ribgrass (*Plantago lanceolata*).
Button weed (*Diodia teres*).
Trumpet creeper (*Campsis radicans*).
Orange hawkweed (*Hieracium aurantiacum*).
Marsh elder (*Iva ciliata*).
Giant ragweed (*Ambrosia trifida*).
Ragweed (*Ambrosia artemisiæfolia*).
Everlasting (*Antennaria* sp.).
Sunflower (*Helianthus* sp.).
Common sunflower (*Helianthus annuus*).
Crownbeard (*Verbesina* sp.).
Beggar ticks (*Bidens* sp.).

MAST AND PINE SEEDS AS FOOD.

Mast, including acorns of the swamp oak (*Quercus palustris*), the white oak (*Q. alba*), beechnuts, the blue beech (*Carpinus caroliniana*), and the chestnut, amounts to 2.47 per cent of the food of the year.

In the pine lands of Florida the bobwhite freely eats the seeds of the long-leaf pine (*Pinus palustris*). Of the 39 birds from Walton County (November, December, and January, 1902 and 1903), 21 had their crops and stomachs mainly filled with this nutritious food. They had usually clipped off the wings of the samaras close to the large seeds. Several crops were full of germinating pine seeds, some of the embryos having cotyledons 2 inches long. In the region about Washington the seeds of the scrub pine (*Pinus virginiana*) also are eaten to a small extent. The fact that these seeds are a good winter food should be remembered by holders of game preserves. Observations show that the key seeds of the maple also are eaten, though much less extensively.

FRUIT AS FOOD.

Unlike the catbird and the cedarbird, whose food consists, respectively, of 50 and 87 per cent of fruit, the food of bobwhite for the year includes only 9.57 per cent of fruit. It is least frugivorous in spring and most so in June and in December and January, taking 20.1 per cent in the summer month and a little over 18 per cent during the two winter months. If more birds collected in June had been available for examination, probably the percentage of fruit would have been lower. The December percentage is evidently characteristic, for it was based on the examination of about 200 stomachs.

In early spring wild winter-cured berries, in May strawberries, later the *Rubus* fruits—thimbleberry, dewberry, and highbush blackberry—and in late summer and autumn an endless profusion of the year's wild harvest yield the bobwhite an accessible and abundant food supply. In late fall and winter, when snow covers the seeds, fruit doubtless keeps it from starving. In December it forms nearly one-fifth of the food for the month. Sumac, wax-myrtle, rose, and bayberry are the main winter supply. Poison-ivy berries are eaten occasionally. Rose hips often project from the snow and furnish timely food. At Falls Church, Va., and at Cabin John Bridge and Marshall Hall, Md., tracks of coveys in deep snow led up to rose shoots to which partly eaten hips were clinging. Sumac and other plants of the genus *Rhus* form 1.60 per cent of the annual food, and during December the proportion of *Rhus* alone is 10.50 per cent. Of 12 birds shot during December at Porters Landing, S. Dak., near the bobwhite's northern limit, by W. C. Colt, each had eaten from 100 to 300 of the carmine sumac berries, and altogether the sumac had furnished 90 per cent of the food they contained. Bayberry and wax-myrtle are as important along the coast as sumacs are inland. Berries of wax-myrtle were found in the stomachs of 15 out of 39 birds collected during November, December, and January, 1902 and 1903, in Walton County, Fla. One hundred and twenty bayberries had been eaten by one bird taken in July, 1901, at Shelter Island, N. Y. Both these fruits last through the winter and well into May, affording excellent provision just when it is most needed.

In spite of its frugivorous tastes and constant association with orchard crops, the bobwhite is not often known to injure cultivated fruits. M. B. Waite reports that near Odenton, Md., it sometimes picks ripening strawberries. Yet birds that were kept in captivity several months refused strawberries when they were hungry. Cultivated cherries were found in a few stomachs, but the bobwhite is not an arboreal feeder and does not damage this crop. During June at Marshall Hall it was repeatedly observed feeding greedily upon the fruit of running dewberry vines. It probably does no serious harm, however, to cultivated bush varieties of *Rubus*, such as the thimbleberry, the raspberry, and the blackberry. It is fond of wild grapes, and a number of crops each contained as many as 25 frost grapes (*Vitis cordifolia*). Hence it might be expected to injure cultivated varieties, for its relative, the California quail, sometimes plunders vineyards; but, so far as the writer knows, vineyards in the East have sustained no appreciable damage from the bobwhite.

In summing up the frugivorous habits of the bobwhite, it may be said that the present investigation shows no appreciable injury to cultivated fruit, but a marked liking for wild fruit. It may be interesting to note, also, that the bobwhite is not nearly so frugivorous as the ruffed grouse.

LIST OF FRUITS EATEN.

Although the percentage of wild fruits yearly consumed is comparatively small, the variety is great, as shown by the appended list, which includes only those actually ascertained to have been eaten. A few careful observers could easily double the number.

Cabbage palmetto (*Inodes palmetto*).
Saw palmetto (*Serenoa serrulata*).
Solomon's seal (*Polygonatum*).
Greenbrier (*Smilax* sp.).
Wax myrtle (*Myrica cerifera*).
Bayberry (*Myrica carolinensis*).
Mulberry (*Morus rubra*).
Sassafras (*Sassafras sassafras*).
Thimbleberry (*Rubus occidentalis*).
High bush blackberry (*Rubus nigrobaccus*).
Dewberry (*Rubus procumbens*).
Strawberry (*Fragaria* sp.).
Rose (*Rosa*).
Haw (*Crataegus* sp.).
Apple (*Malus malus*).
Cultivated cherry (*Prunus* sp.).
Wild cherry (*Prunus serotina*).
Poison ivy (*Rhus radicans*).
Dwarf sumac (*Rhus copallina*).
Staghorn sumac (*Rhus hirta*).
Smooth scarlet sumac (*Rhus glabra*).
Holly (*Ilex opaca*).
Black alder (*Ilex verticillata*).
Climbing bittersweet (*Celastrus scandens*).
Frost grape (*Vitis cordifolia*).
Flowering dogwood (*Cornus florida*).
Sour gum (*Nyssa sylvatica*).
Wintergreen (*Gaultheria procumbens*).
Huckleberry (*Gaylussacia* sp.).
Blueberry (*Vaccinium* sp.).
Ground-cherry (*Physalis pubescens*).
Nightshade (*Solanum nigrum*).
Elder (*Sambucus canadensis*).
Black haw (*Viburnum prunifolium*).
Honeysuckle (*Lonicera* sp.).
Partridge berry (*Mitchella repens*).
Sarsaparilla (*Aralia*).
Woodbine (*Parthenocissus quinquefolia*).

LEAVES AND BUDS AS FOOD.

The bobwhite does not approach the ruffed grouse in destructiveness to leaves, buds, and tender shoots, though occasionally it samples them. It eats the leaves of sorrel sometimes, both yellow sorrel (*Oxalis stricta*) and red sorrel (*Rumex acetosella*). It has been known to take the leaves of cinquefoil (*Potentilla*), and is extremely fond of both red and white clover. Captive birds ate grass, lettuce, and chickweed.

INSECTS AS FOOD.

Notwithstanding statements to the contrary, published and unpublished, the bobwhite eats insects in every month of the year. They form 15.05 per cent of its entire food for the year. From June to August, inclusive, when insects are most numerous, their proportion in the food is 35.97 per cent. The variety of insect food is large.

In the present investigation 116 species have been noted, and further study will doubtless greatly increase the number. Moreover, the large proportion of injurious insects habitually eaten renders the services of this bird more valuable than those of many birds whose percentage of insect food, though greater, includes a smaller proportion of injurious species. Conspicuous among the pests destroyed are the Colorado potato beetle, twelve-spotted cucumber beetle, bean leaf-beetle, squash ladybird, wireworms and their beetle, and May beetles. Its food also includes such weevils as corn billbugs, imbricated snout beetle, clover leaf weevil, cotton boll weevil; also the striped garden caterpillar, army worm, cotton bollworm, and various species of cutworms; also the corn-louse ants, red-legged grasshopper, Rocky Mountain locust, and chinch bug. The bobwhite does not merely sample these species, as do many other birds; it eats some of them in considerable numbers, for crops examined have contained, respectively, a dozen cutworms, an equal number of army worms, 30 Rocky Mountain locusts, and 47 cotton boll weevils. This bird also destroys striped cucumber beetles by the score, potato beetles by the hundred, and chinch bugs in great numbers. From June to August, inclusive, insects and their allies form, as previously mentioned, about a third of the food. Of this beetles make up nearly half, or 15.37 per cent; bugs, 8.54 per cent; caterpillars, 1.37 per cent; grasshoppers, 6.93 per cent; miscellaneous insects, 1.33 per cent, and spiders, with other invertebrates, 2.43 per cent.

BEETLES EATEN.

The beetles most largely destroyed are ground beetles, leaf-eating beetles, and weevils. Naturally, because of the terrestrial habits of the bobwhite, ground beetles, in spite of their vile odor and irritating secretions, are picked up oftener than the other kinds. Experiments with caged birds prove that even the most pungent forms are relished. Ground beetles are numerous in species and superabundant in individuals. One can form no adequate idea of their numbers except at night. Arc lights kill them by thousands. The writer has known one species (*Harpalus pennsylvanicus*) to enter open windows in the evening in swarms. They have an irritating secretion, which if applied to the skin soon raises a blister. Ground beetles are more or less predaceous, hence the whole family was formerly considered beneficial. Later study has resulted in their division into three classes: The most carnivorous species, possessing sharp, curved jaws for capturing and killing other insects; the least predaceous forms, having blunt jaws and eating considerable vegetable matter; and a class intermediate between these two. The first class contains highly beneficial beetles which destroy great numbers of insect pests, while the blunt-jawed class includes some injurious species that feed on crops. Only a few of the bobwhite stomachs examined contained the useful sharp-jawed beetles, but many contained the blunt-jawed species, especially such forms as *Amara* sp., *Agonoderus pallipes, Anisodactylus baltimorensis, Anisodactylus rusticus, Harpalus pennsylvanicus,* and *Harpalus caliginosus.* At Marshall Hall, in August, 1902, a covey of bobwhites was seen greedily eating beetles of the two species of *Harpalus* named above, which were numerous in wheat stubble overgrown by ragweed. The meadow lark, also, was feeding on them. The liking of the bobwhite for *Harpalus pennsylvanicus* was further proved by experiments with caged birds. It eats also the larvæ of these beetles, as do the robin and several other birds. Though the genus *Harpalus* as a whole is useful, destruction of these two species is not amiss, for they injure ripening strawberries by eating out the seeds. Through their depredations on a quarter-acre patch a grower at Leesburg, Va., in three nights lost $350 worth of fruit. The nature of the injury by the beetle has so far made remedial measures impracticable; therefore, the work of the bobwhite and other birds should be estimated at its full value.

Leaf-eating beetles, next in importance after ground beetles in the diet of the bobwhite, include many of the worst beetle pests, and members of the family not already actively injurious are potentially so. These beetles also are provided with protective secretions, more effectively repellant in the larger species, at least, than those of ground beetles, but luckily ineffectual against bobwhite. He eats the most injurious of these insects, such as the potato beetle (*Leptinotarsa decemlineata*), the striped cucumber beetle (*Diabrotica vittata*), the twelve-spotted cucumber beetle (*Diabrotica 12-punctata*), and the squash ladybird (*Epilachna borealis*). The first named is perhaps more correctly termed the Colorado potato beetle. It was a native of the Rocky Mountains originally, feeding on the horse-nettle (*Solanum rostratum*), a plant related to the potato. It began to migrate eastward a year or two before the civil war, and fifteen or sixteen years later reached the Atlantic coast. Since then, as every one knows, this beetle has threatened the potato crop of the country. Birds as a rule avoid it because of its secretions. Therefore the bobwhite's services in destroying it should be highly valued, the more so because the bird's habit of eating the potato bug is not merely occasional nor limited to special localities. Records have come to the Biological Survey from New Jersey, Virginia, Maryland, Iowa, Kansas, Nebraska, Texas, and Ontario; and it is believed that more extended observations will show that the habit is general wherever the birds and the beetles inhabit the same district. During the last week of June, at Marshall Hall, a pair of birds was observed patroling rows of badly infested potato vines and diligently picking off the beetles. Writing of the bird's relation to this insect, C. E.

Romaine, of Crockett, Tex., says: "Quail have built their nests around my fence and even in my garden, within 50 feet of my house. They have kept my potato patch entirely free from the Colorado potato bug." Three captive bobwhites dispatched 50 potato beetles in five minutes, swallowing them whole, apparently with great zest. No food offered them was eaten with more avidity. Thomas McIlwraith says a recent writer mentions that he examined the crop of one which was killed as it rose from a potato patch and found that it contained 75 potato bugs.[a] Lawrence Bruner reports 101 of these beetles found in a single crop.[b] Such wholesale destruction of these pests throughout a large territory is an invaluable aid to agriculture.

The two species of cucumber beetles (*Diabrotica vittata* and *D. 12-punctata*) are highly injurious to cucumbers, squashes, melons, and corn, much of the harm being caused by their larvæ, which feed on the roots of infested crops and are difficult to combat successfully with insecticides. The bobwhite eats them freely without ill effect, though examination seldom reveals them in the stomachs of other birds. Indeed, captive birds of all the other species experimented with have refused them, probably because of their offensive secretions.

To some extent the bobwhite feeds also on certain leaf beetles, known, from their jumping powers, as flea beetles. Its favorites appear to be the three-lined potato beetle (*Lema trilineata*), sometimes an ally of the potato beetle in the potato patch, *Œdionychus fimbriata*, and several members of the genus *Disonycha*. The golden tortoise beetle (*Coptocycla bicolor*), an insect that looks like a drop of molten gold and is an enemy of the sweet potato, is also eaten. The locust leaf-mining beetle (*Odontota dorsalis*) is another victim of the bird. Its larvæ tunnel between the surfaces of locust leaves and kill the foliage. In 1895 the ravages of this pest turned the locust-fringed bluffs on the Potomac below Washington as brown as if touched by fire.

The agriculturist finds weevils hard to cope with, on account of their small size, protective coloration, and retiring mode of life. Birds, however, destroy them in large numbers, often a score or two at a meal, and bobwhite does his share of the work. He often eats two common species that feed on clover leaves (*Sitones hispidulus* and *Phytonomus punctatus*), and preys also on the two billbugs (*Sphenophorus parvulus* and *Sphenophorus zeæ*), the latter injurious to corn. He relishes also that notorious garden pest, the imbricated snout beetle. His most important weevil prey is the Mexican cotton boll weevil (*Anthonomus grandis*). In 1894 this insect first crossed the Mexican border into Texas. During 1903 it caused a loss of

---

[a] Birds of Ontario, p. 170, 1894.   [b] Notes on Nebraska Birds, p. 80, 1896.

$15,000,000. Though still chiefly confined to Texas, in time it will undoubtedly occupy the whole cotton belt and do a tremendous amount of harm. The bobwhite is fond of this pest. F. M. Howard, of Beeville, Tex., in writing to the Bureau of Entomology, says that the crops of bobwhites shot at Beeville, Tex., were filled with these weevils.[a] H. G. Wood, of Cuero, Tex., in a letter dated September 21, 1901, relating to the weevil scourge, says:

Several of our business men and farmers are of the opinion that the quail can be made a vehicle for the destruction of the cotton boll weevil. One farmer reports his cotton fields full of quail. and the entire absence of weevils. He found 47 weevils in the craw of one bird. * * * I claim quail are the greatest insect destroyers of all birds. * * * We propose to prohibit the killing of quail in this county this season. hoping thereby to save a great portion of the cotton crop next season.

The click beetles, the larvæ of which are the wireworms so inimical to corn and other plants of the grass family; *scarabœid* beetles, though in smaller numbers; dung beetles, when numerous, and May beetles, parents of the injurious white grub, are eaten by the bobwhite. The May beetle (*Lachnosterna* sp.) and its near relative, *Ligyrus gibbosus*, were eagerly eaten by captive birds. The useful ladybirds (*Coccinellidæ*) are sometimes found in the bird's crop, but, judging from experiments with caged birds, do not appear to be highly relished. *Adalia bipunctata* was several times offered and refused, but was finally eaten. The one harmful beetle of the family, the squash ladybird (*Epilachna borealis*), has been found in stomachs and was relished by captive birds. Certain miscellaneous beetles belonging to different families are occasionally picked up, such as rove beetles, soldier beetles, darkling beetles, histerid beetles, and longicorn beetles.

LIST OF BEETLES EATEN.

The beetles known to be eaten by the bobwhite include the following:

GROUND BEETLES (Carabidæ):
Scarites subterraneus.
Amara sp.
Casnonia pennsylvanica.
Platynus extensicollis.
Agonoderus pallipes.
Harpalus pennsylvanicus.
Harpalus calignosus.
Anisodactylus rusticus.
Anisodactylus baltimorensis.
LEAF BEETLES (Chrysomelidæ):
Lema trilineata.
Cryptocephalus venustus.
Colaspis brunnea.

LEAF BEETLES—Continued.
Nodonota tristis.
Leptinotarsa decemlineata (potato beetle).
Chrysomela pulchra.
Chrysomela suturalis.
Cerotoma trifurcata (bean leaf-beetle).
Diabrotica vittata (striped cucumber beetle).
Diabrotica 12-punctata (twelve-spotted cucumber beetle).
Œdionychis fimbriata.
Disonycha 5-vittata.

---

[a] Circular 27, new series, Division of Entomology, p. 6, 1897.

LEAF BEETLES—Continued.
Disonycha xanthomelæna.
Disonycha crenicollis.
Psylliodes punctulata.
Microrhopala vittata.
Odontota dorsalis (locust leaf-mining beetle).
Coptocycla bicolor (golden tortoise beetle).
MAY BEETLES (Scarabæidæ) :
Onthophagus pennsylvanicus (dung beetle).
Aphodius inguinatus (dung beetle).
Serica sp.
Diplotaxis sp. (leaf-chafer).
Lachnosterna tristis (May beetle).
Anomala sp.
Aphonus sp.
SNOUT BEETLES (suborder Rhynchophora) :
Thecesternus humeralis.
Epicærus imbricatus (imbricated snout beetle).
Tanymecus confertus.
Aramigus fulleri (Fuller's rose beetle).
Sitones hispidulus (clover weevil).
Phytonomus punctatus (clover-leaf weevil).

SNOUT BEETLES—Continued.
Anthonomus grandis (Mexican cotton boll weevil).
Chalcodermus collaris.
Centrinus sp.
Sphenophorus parvulus (billbug).
Sphenophorus zeæ (corn billbug).
CLICK BEETLES (Elateridæ) :
Drasterius elegans.
Agriotes sp.
Melanotus communis.
Corymbites sp.
LADYBIRDS (Coccinellidæ) :
Hippodamia parenthesis.
Coccinella sanguinea.
Adalia bipunctata.
Epilachna borealis (squash ladybird).
HISTERID BEETLES (Histeridæ).
DARKLING BEETLES (Tenebrionidæ) :
Blapstinus.
ROVE BEETLES (Staphylinidæ).
SOLDIER BEETLES (Lampyridæ) :
Chauliognathus pennsylvanicus.
LONGICORN BEETLES (Cerambycidæ) :
Tetraopes tetraophthalmus.

BUGS EATEN.

The bobwhite eats comparatively more bugs than most birds, including both *Heteroptera*, or true bugs, and *Homoptera*, which form 2.77 per cent of its food. The maximum number of bugs was taken in August and amounted to 21.1 per cent of the food for that month.

The chinch bug, which in this country has destroyed over $100,000,-000 worth of wheat and other cereals in a season, is preyed upon by the bobwhite throughout the year. C. V. Riley says: " In the winter time, when hard pushed for food, this bird must devour immense numbers of the little pests, which winter in just such situations as are frequented by the quail; and this bird should be protected from the gun of the sportsman in every State where the chinch bug is known to run riot." [a] The data possessed by the Biological Survey concerning this species are scanty, but they show that the quail destroys the pest in Ohio, Indiana, Illinois, Missouri, Kansas, and Nebraska. The number of chinch bugs eaten varies, but usually appears to be large. Thus a bird shot October 12, 1901, at Badger, Nebr., by W. C. Colt, had picked up 100, and the American Field for February

---

[a] Missouri Reports, II, p. 28, 1870.

21, 1903, reports that an observer at Seymour, Ind., found a teaspoonful in a crop. In a letter to the Department of Agriculture, M. A. Page, of Garnett, Kans., says of a bobwhite: " On opening the crop we found about two tablespoonfuls of chinch bugs."

The bobwhite also destroys the false chinch bug (*Nysius angustatus*), which attacks grapes, strawberries, apples, potatoes, turnips, radishes, beets, and cabbages. It eats the tarnished plant bug (*Lygus pratensis*), injurious to fruit and truck crops, and stink bugs of more than a dozen species, one (*Euschistus variolarius*) being a pest on many garden vegetables. The noninjurious species, particularly *Thyanta custator*, are often eaten, one bird containing 30 of them. More *Homoptera* (leaf hoppers and other forms) are eaten by bobwhite than by most other birds. The little leaf hopper (*Oncometopia lateralis*) is especially relished.

LIST OF BUGS EATEN.

HETEROPTERA :
- *Blissus leucopterus* (chinch bug).
- *Nysius angustatus* (false chinch bug).
- *Euschistus tristigmus* (three-spotted soldier bug).
- *Euschistus variolarius.*
- *Euschistus* sp.
- *Podisus* sp.
- *Brochymena* sp.
- *Nezara hilaris.*
- *Mormidea lugens.*
- *Hymenarcys nervosa.*
- *Hymenarcys æqualis.*
- *Thyanta custator.*
- *Œbalus pugnax.*
- *Trichopepla semivittata.*

HETEROPTERA—Continued.
- *Cœnus delius.*
- *Peribalus limbolarius.*
- *Lygus pratensis* (tarnished plant bug).
- *Corimelæna* sp.
- *Apiomerus crassipes.*
- *Alydus eurinus.*
- *Corizus* sp.
- *Euthoctha galeator.*
- *Scutelleridæ* (shield-backed bugs).

HOMOPTERA :
- *Oncometopia lateralis.*
- *Oncometopia* sp.
- *Deltocephalus* sp.
- *Diedrocephala* sp.

GRASSHOPPERS AND ALLIED INSECTS EATEN.

Grasshoppers with a few crickets make 3.71 per cent of the yearly food. In September they contribute 11.9 per cent. The walking stick, singularly like a twig and at times very numerous and injurious to foliage of shade and forest trees, has been found in the stomach of the bobwhite. Locusts and meadow grasshoppers, both highly destructive to vegetation, are favorite articles of diet. The bird grasshopper, so called from its size, is occasionally eaten. The destructive grasshoppers or locusts of the genus *Melanoplus*, such as *M. atlanis*, *M. femur-rubrum*, or the red-legged grasshopper, and the Rocky Mountain locust, form the bulk of the orthopterous food of the species. The Rocky Mountain locust is one of the worst of insect pests, and its appearance in large numbers is a calamity. It appears in swarms, clouding the sun and covering the earth, sweeping every green thing before it, and often driving the farmer from home and threatening him with starvation. During a single season it has caused a loss of $100,000,000.

In 1874–75 Samuel Aughey made a special study of a Nebraska invasion and found that the bobwhites were an active enemy of the locusts. Of 21 birds shot between May and October, inclusive, all but five had fed on locusts. The smallest number taken by any bird was 20 and the largest 39; in all, 539—an average of 25 apiece. C. V. Riley ascertained that the bird feeds also on the eggs of the locust, particularly in winter, when they are exposed by the freezing and thawing of the ground. If every covey destroyed as many locusts in a day as the one just referred to, it is hard to overestimate the usefulness of the bobwhite where abundant in infested regions.

The following are a few of the many species of orthopterous insects identified from the crops and stomachs of bobwhites:

Cricket (*Gryllus* sp.).
Meadow grasshoppers (*Xiphidium, Orchelinum, Scudderia*).
Katydid (*Microcentrum* sp.).
Walking sticks (*Phasmidæ*).
Grouse locust (*Tettix* sp.).
Mountain locust (*Melanoplus spretus*).

Red-legged grasshopper (*Melanoplus femur-rubrum*).
Grasshopper (*Melanoplus bivittatus, M. scudderi, M. atlanis*).
Bird grasshopper (*Schistocerca americana*).

CATERPILLARS EATEN.

The bobwhite seems to eat fewer caterpillars than would be expected from its terrestrial habits. The yearly proportion only formed 0.95 per cent and the maximum quantity eaten in a month was 4 per cent in May. This apparent neglect of caterpillars as food is perhaps due to their scarcity where the birds for the present study were shot. Pupæ and adult moths occasionally serve as food. Whatever the list of species of caterpillars eaten by bobwhite lacks in length it makes up in importance, for so great a proportion of serious lepidopterous pests is seldom found in the fare of any bird. As is true of some other birds, the bobwhite includes the army worm in its bill of fare. This pest sometimes exists in legions and moves steadily forward from field to field, devouring corn, oats, forage, and other crops. Fortunately it is not often active, and the years of its occurrence are frequently separated by long intervals. Every year, however, the different species of cutworms do serious damage. They cut down germinating grain, often before the plants have fairly sprung above ground. Owing to their mode of feeding, a few worms may lop off many plants in a night. It seems strange that the bobwhites find as many of these nocturnal larvæ as they do. The cotton worm, a pest so destructive that in one year it has caused a loss of $30,000,000 to the cotton fields, is preyed upon by the bobwhite. Tobacco worms were sparingly eaten by bobwhites at Marshall Hall, but experiments indicated that they may eat them in greater numbers when opportunity offers. Five tobacco worms (*Phlegethontius sexta*), two-thirds grown, placed in a cage with three captive bobwhites, July 8, 1903, were devoured in less than two minutes. Cabbage worms (*Pontia rapæ*) and cutworms also were offered and greedily eaten.

LIST OF CATERPILLARS EATEN.

Army worm (*Heliophila unipuncta*).
Cutworm (*Agrotis* sp.).
Cutworm (*Feltia annexa*).
Noctuid moth (*Noctuidæ*).
Cotton worm (*Alabama argillacea*).
Cotton bollworm (*Heliothis obsoleta*).
Striped garden caterpillar (*Manestra legitima*).
Yellow bear caterpillar (*Diacrisia virginica*).
Pyralid (*Tholeria reversalis*).
Purslane sphinx (*Deilephila gallii*).
Southern tobacco worm (*Phlegethontius sexta*).
Caterpillar (*Junonia cœnia*).
Pupa (*Vanessa* sp.).

MISCELLANEOUS ANIMAL FOOD.

Insects of several orders not previously mentioned make up 0.70 per cent of the food of the bobwhite. They include hymenopterous insects, such as ants (*Lasius* sp., *Tetramorium cæspitum*, *Camponotus pennsylvanicus*); gall flies (*Cynipidæ*), which produce bladderlike growths on plants; in rare instances parasitic wasps (*Tiphia inornata* and *Proctotrypes rufipes*); crane flies, May flies, and sometimes true flies, like the green fly (*Lucilia cæsar*) and the robber fly (*Asilidæ*). The animal food of the bird includes other orders besides insects. The greater part of this is spiders, chiefly ground spiders, with a few harvest spiders (*Phalangidæ*). The common thousand leg (*Julus* sp.) sometimes contributes to the food, as it often does to that of many species of song birds. Snails are more often taken. Among these *Pupa armifera* and the pond snail (*Succinea avara*) have been identified. The little fresh-water lobster called crayfish (*Cambarus*) had furnished the major course for 4 out of 15 birds shot by collectors for S. A. Forbes in Illinois. Manipulation of these biting crustaceans would appear to be difficult for a bird no larger than bobwhite. The queerest food eaten is the toad. B. H. Warren reported Florida birds as feeding on small batrachians (probably young toads), and laboratory examination of Florida birds showed in one case a tiny toad. It is fortunate that this habit of bobwhite is not general, since the toad is useful and destroys great numbers of insects.

FOOD OF THE YOUNG.

During the breeding season a third of the food of adult bobwhites consists of insects, while their young, like those of practically all other land birds, consume a much greater proportion of insect food than do their parents. At Marshall Hall, July 24, 19 droppings collected from two broods of downy chicks—one but a few hours out of the shell and the other probably several days old—consisted wholly of the remains of insects. Their fragmentary condition made the species almost unrecognizable, but the following were identified:

Minute green leaf-eating beetles (*Chrysomelidæ*), at least two species.

Leaf-eating beetle (*Colaspis brunnea*).

Small scarabæid beetles (*Scarabæidæ*), two species.

Longicorn beetle (*Cerambycidæ*), one species.

Ground beetles (*Carabidæ*), five species.

Weevils (*Rhynchophora*).

Grasshopper (*Acrididæ*).

Caterpillars (*Lepidoptera*).

Ants (*Formicidæ*).

Stink bug (*Euschistus?*).

Spiders (*Arachnida*).

Thousand legs (*Julus* sp.).

MASKED BOBWHITE.

(*Colinus ridgwayi.*)

The masked bobwhite is slightly smaller than the bobwhite of the Eastern States, and the male differs strikingly, having the chin, throat, and sides of the head black, and the underside of the body usually uniform rusty reddish. Since the discovery of the bird little has been added to our knowledge of its life history beyond some notes on its distribution, and the fact of its probable extinction within our borders. It lived on grassy plains covering a limited area in southern Arizona, south and southwest of Tucson, and ranged into northern Sonora, Mexico. In regard to the causes leading to the disappearance of the masked bobwhite, Herbert Brown writes as follows:

The causes leading to the extermination of the Arizona masked bobwhite (*Colinus ridgwayi*) are due to the overstocking of the country with cattle, supplemented by several rainless years. This combination practically stripped the country bare of vegetation. Of their range the *Colinus* occupied only certain restricted portions, and when their food and shelter had been trodden out of existence by thousands of hunger-dying stock, there was nothing left for poor little bobwhite to do but go out with them. As the conditions in Sonora were similar to those in Arizona, birds and cattle suffered in common. The Arizona bobwhite would have thriven well in an agricultural country, in brushy fence corners, tangled thickets, and weed-covered fields, but such things were not to be had in their habitat. Unless a few can still be found on the Upper Santa Cruz we can, in truth, bid them a final good-by.[a]

Recent information received by the Biological Survey from Sonora is to the effect that these interesting birds still survive in parts of that region, and efforts are being made by a game association to obtain living birds from there to introduce into California. The natural home of the masked bobwhite, in the hot and arid desert of southern

---

[a] Auk., XXI, p. 213, April, 1904.

Arizona and northern Sonora, is sufficient guaranty that the birds would thrive in cultivated sections anywhere in southern California and the arid Southwest. It would be deplorable if so handsome and useful a bird should be allowed to become extinct, and a determined effort should be made to introduce it into suitable localities before it is too late.

Beyond what Herbert Brown has stated we have practically nothing on this bird's habits. He has told us that, like all the birds of the genus *Colinus*, the males give the well-known ' bobwhite ' call, and he translates their rallying note as ' hoo-we.' He examined the stomachs of three birds. The first contained mustard seed, chaparral berries, six or eight beetles, and other insects; the second only a single grasshopper an inch long, and the third contained 20 ants, several crescent-shaped seeds, and a large number of small, fleshy green leaves.

It is stated by Bendire that in Sonora Benson found these birds only in fields where wheat and barley had been grown. Probably then the bird's general habits may be safely assumed to be similar to those of its relative, bobwhite.

CALIFORNIA QUAIL.

(*Lophortyx californicus.*)[a]

The California quail is generally dispersed over California below an altitude of 8,000 feet and extends into southern Oregon and western Nevada. It has been introduced into Washington and British Columbia, and efforts to introduce it into the Hawaiian Islands also have proved very successful, although of late years its numbers there have been much reduced by the mongoose, by which in time it is likely to be exterminated. Two geographic forms of the bird are recognized, a dark form and a light one, but as they do not differ in habits they are not distinguished in the following account. It is a beautiful bird with a most pleasing combination of colors and markings, its head being adorned by a glossy black crest, narrow at the base and gradually widening into gracefully recurving plumes, and the markings on the underparts resembling scales. It frequents brush-covered hillsides, canyons, thickets along water courses and the borders of roads, as well as vineyards and other cultivated fields. The nesting time of the species varies considerably according to locality and conditions. According to E. A. Mearns it nests in March and April in Ventura County, Cal. Nests containing eggs were found

---

[a] This name is used here to cover both the typical California quail (*Lophortyx californicus*) and the paler, more southerly form, called the valley quail (*L. c. vallicola*).

during the last week of May in Tulare County, Cal., by J. E. McLellan. The eggs usually number 12 to 15, and are white or buff with spots.

These birds take kindly to civilization, and flocks are not rarely seen in the suburbs of large towns, where they range through the gardens and orchards. They often nest close to farm buildings, and W. Otto Emerson states that a pair nested within a rod of his front door, though nearly every hour people and vehicles were passing within four feet of the nest.

Instead of spending the night in a circle on the ground, like the bobwhite, the California quail chooses much safer places and roosts in bushes or low thickly foliaged trees. This quail is even more confiding than the bobwhite, and frequently comes about farm buildings to eat with the chickens. It has been known to lay in confinement, and appears to yield readily to semidomestication.

The valley quail has acquired the interesting habit of posting sentinels when feeding, which is described in detail by John J. Williams. Mr. Williams observed a flock enter a field and begin to feed, while a sentinel took his station in a peach tree and scanned the country round about for danger. Presently he was relieved by a second bird, who took up a position on a brush pile and a little later was relieved by a third, who kept guard while the other two fed with the flock.[a]

Writing in 1891 Clark P. Streator says that about 100,000 are sold each year in the San Francisco market. It is not a perfect game bird, for it does not lie well to a dog, and when once flushed has a habit of running that is exasperating to the sportsman. The best way to hunt these quail is to keep the dog at heel and to run down the birds. This is likely to make them take wing and to break up the covey. The same result may be accomplished also by discharging the gun in the air. When a covey has been scattered in suitable cover they will lie well enough to a trained dog to give the hunter considerable sport, though it is poor in comparison with that afforded by the bobwhite. The beauty of this quail, its pleasant call notes, and its confidence in man make it a favorite, except where it damages the grape crop. In fall and winter where it is abundant hundreds of birds unite in great packs. Bendire, writing in 1892, says that within a decade packs of 500 were often found, but that at that time coveys even of 50 were rare in most places.[b] In the fall of 1891 they were still very abundant on the west side of the San Joaquin Valley, where E. W. Nelson, of the Biological Survey, records their slaughter by pot hunters. The hunters stationed themselves behind a brush blind near the one spring where the birds came to drink. Thousands of them flocked

---

[a] Condor, vol. 5, pp. 146–148, 1903.
[b] Life Hist. N. Am. Birds [I], p. 24, 1892.

thither for water during the day, and by waiting until many birds were bunched the hunters killed at least a score at each discharge of the gun. In a week of this butchery 8,400 quails were killed. A record of 525 birds to four guns in a day in February, 1903, near San Diego, Cal., shows that birds are still abundant there, though far less numerous in most places than formerly.[a]

The California quail, though not a large consumer of insects, is a useful bird, since weed seeds constitute more than half of its food. In some regions these birds suffer from the curtailment of their food supply by droughts, and in the northern part of their range many are killed by severe winters. Bendire states that during the excessively cold winter of 1887–88, when the mercury dropped to 28° below zero in the northeastern corner of California, these quail perished in great numbers.[b]

The California quail might be introduced successfully in many sections between California and Texas where it does not occur at present. It already has been introduced into Colorado, where it will be protected by law at all seasons until 1920. Laws to prevent trapping and to limit the day's bag, together with absolute protection in sections where necessary, should suffice to preserve this beautiful species.

FOOD HABITS.

The general food habits of this quail have been ascertained by the examination of 601 stomachs, and it proves to be one of the most largely vegetarian of game birds. The material for investigation was collected in California, and represents every month of the year except May. Insects furnished but 2.15 per cent of the food, and leaves, seeds, and fruit 97.85 per cent.

INSECT AND OTHER ANIMAL FOOD.

The 2.15 per cent of animal food eaten by this quail is distributed as follows: Spiders, 0.03 per cent; beetles, 0.22 per cent; grasshoppers and crickets, 0.24 per cent; ants and other Hymenoptera, 0.67 per cent; miscellaneous insects, 0.99 per cent. The beetles are both adults and larvæ, and belong to the following families: *Chrysomelidæ* (leaf-eating beetles), *Tenebrionidæ* (darkling beetles), *Elateridæ* (wireworms), *Carabidæ* (ground beetles), *Dermestidæ* (dermestids), *Coccinellidæ* (ladybirds), and snout beetles (suborder *Rhynchophora*). The leaf-eating beetles include *Diabrotica soror*, a western representative of the destructive twelve-spotted cucumber beetle. Flea beetles also are eaten, including species of the genus *Haltica*. Among the

---

[a] Recreation, vol. 18, p. 368, 1893.
[b] Life Hist. N. Am. Birds [I], p. 26, 1892.

miscellaneous leaf-eating beetles may be mentioned the brilliant *Gastroidea cæsia*. Conspicuous among the ground beetles eaten is the common *Agonoderus pallipes*, and among the useful predaceous ladybirds the species *Hippodamia convergens*. Like the eastern bobwhite, the California quail feeds on ants of the families *Formicidæ* and *Myrmicidæ*. Sometimes 20 to 35 ants are taken at a meal. Of the other Hymenoptera, gall insects (*Cynipidæ*) and their galls make a significant proportion. Caterpillars and their pupæ are eaten. Cutworms (*Agrotis*), measuring worms (*Geometridæ*), sphinx caterpillars (including *Deilephila*), and the cotton bollworm (*Heliothis obsoleta*) make up the greater part of this food. Like the bobwhite again, this bird shows a relish for bugs. It eats leaf bugs (*Capsidæ*), bugs of the chinch bug family, such as *Lygæus truculentis* and *L. bitriangularis*, and stink bugs (*Pentatomidæ*), assassin bugs (*Reduviidæ*), flat bugs (*Aradidæ*), burrower bugs (*Crytomenus*), leaf hoppers (*Jassidæ*), tree hoppers (*Membracidæ*), plant lice, and bugs of the genus *Scolops* (*Fulgoridæ*). The miscellaneous animal matter taken includes flies (*Lucillia cæsar*), spiders, and snails.

VEGETABLE FOOD.

FRUIT.

The vegetable food of this quail amounts to 97.85 per cent of its diet. The bird has an unsavory reputation among fruit growers, especially the owners of vineyards. Relative to this subject, Miss Florence A. Merriam, writing from San Diego County, Cal., says:

In fact, the quail were so abundant as to be a pest. For several years great flocks of them came down the canyons to Major Merriam's vineyard, where they destroyed annually from twenty to thirty tons of fruit. In one season—July to October, 1881—one hundred and thirty dozen [1,560] were trapped on his ranch. The result of this wholesale destruction was manifest when I returned to the valley in 1894. The birds were then rarely seen on the roads and seldom flushed in riding about the valley.[a]

When this species becomes superabundant and plays havoc with crops it is well to remember that it can be so easily checked. W. H. Osgood, of the Biological Survey, has furnished the writer data on the frugivorous habits of the quail in central California. In one vineyard he saw a flock of about a thousand eating zinfandel grapes. The birds do much damage in September, when the young are molting and they have collected in packs, as before described.

Walter E. Bryant, writing of the damage to fruit, offers testimony on the other side:

In some parts of California there is a strong prejudice against the quail, owing to alleged damage to the grape. The evidence which I have thus far gathered shows that the quail do pick at the bunches of grapes, and not alone

---

[a] Auk, XIII, p. 116, 1896.

those bunches which are near or on the ground; but the damage which they cause seems overestimated. Too often mutilated bunches of grapes are supposed to be due to the presence of quail in the vineyard; but there are other birds and mammals, also, which vary their diet with grapes. I have examined a number of quail's crops and gizzards without finding the presence of grapes, although the birds had been shot near and in vineyards. A quail's crop sent to me from Los Gatos, by Mr. A. H. Hawley, contained twenty-five small grapes; others had a few grapes, seeds, and poison-oak berries.[a]

In the 601 stomachs of the valley quail examined by the Biological Survey grapes formed only 0.01 per cent of the annual food. This small quantity is due, no doubt, to the fact that many of the birds were shot in regions remote from vineyards and many of them during the time when grapes were not in fruit. The total proportion of all kinds of fruit was only 7.60 per cent, an amount so insignificant as to preclude the idea of serious damage. Where the birds are over-abundant and the consequent damage great, trapping or advertising the conditions in sporting papers will probably result in reducing the numbers to normal. Of the 7.60 per cent of fruit, grapes, as before stated, contribute 0.01 per cent; plants of the genus *Rhus*, mainly *Rhus diversiloba*, 4.74 per cent, and miscellaneous fruit, prunes, and vaccinium, 2.85 per cent. The maximum quantity of fruit, amounting to 32.40 per cent for the month, was taken in December, after the grapes had been picked.

GRAIN.

The relations of the California quail to grain are of considerable economic importance. W. T. Craig, of San Francisco, writes to the Department of Agriculture: " I have observed the quail enter a field of wheat to the number of thousands, and had they not been driven away they would have destroyed the whole crop." No other reports to the Biological Survey show the danger to grain from this quail to be so serious, but data at hand show that it does more or less damage to germinating grain. Two quail shot by Walter E. Bryant on a newly-sown grain field had eaten, respectively, 185 kernels and 210 kernels of barley.[b] Barley is important in California, where it is grown for hay, for grain feed, and for beer making. There is, however, much volunteer barley, which many species of birds feed on and thus do good rather than harm. It is probable that quail do little or no harm to barley at harvest time, and the waste grain that they subsequently gather in stubble fields has no positive value. Of the yearly food of the 601 quail examined 6.18 per cent was grain, divided as follows: Barley, 4.58 per cent; wheat, 0.44 per cent; corn and oats, 1.16 per cent.

---

a Zoe, IV, p, 56, 1893,   b Zoe, IV, p. 55, 1893,

LEAVES.

In its habit of feeding on foliage the California quail differs from the bobwhite and resembles the ruffed grouse. Such food forms 22.73 per cent of the vegetable matter eaten. In February, when the bobwhite is weathering blizzards, the California quail is enjoying balmy weather and feeding on browse to the extent of 80 per cent of its food. Most of this browse consists of leaves of leguminous plants, principally clovers. Bur clover (*Medicago denticulata*), a weed that grows in cultivated land and along irrigation ditches, appears to supply most of the forage. Alfalfa and clovers of the genus alfalfa form most of the remaining leguminous green food. Next to legumes the finely divided leaves of alfilaria, or ' filaree ' (*Erodium*), are important. Grass, chickweed (*Alsine media*), the leaves of fern, geranium, oxalis, and groundsel-bush (*Baccharis*) also furnish forage for the quail. W. W. Cooke reports that near Grand Junction, Colo., where the California coast quail has been introduced and thrives wonderfully, market gardeners regard it as a nuisance.[a]

WEED SEEDS.

Different seeds, largely of weeds, furnish the California quail 59.77 per cent of its year's diet. Legumes contribute 17.87 per cent; alfilaria, 13.38 per cent; compositæ, 5.55 per cent; the spurge family (*Euphorbiaceæ*), 5.85 per cent, and miscellaneous plants 17.12 per cent. Leguminous seeds are liked best by the bird, and make up 17.87 per cent of the seed diet for the year and 46.1 per cent of its food for June. Bur clover yields abundance of seeds as well as forage. Its seed pod is peculiar, much elongated, beset with long, sharp spines, and spirally coiled into a roundish bur. The quail swallows it whole, regardless of spines. This food is highly nutritious and is relished by stock as well as by birds and wild mammals. Seeds of closely allied plants, such as alfalfa, vetch, cassias, cultivated beans and peas, and clovers of the genera *Trifolium*, *Lespedeza*, and *Melilotus* also are in the quail's list, as well as of locust (*Robinia*) and lupines, the latter taken in large quantities. They include the seeds of *Lupinus nanus*, *L. micranthus*, and *L. sparsiflorus*. Other leguminous seeds are eaten in great numbers, including a small bean-like seed, *Lotus glaber*, which looks much like a miniature Frankfurt sausage, and an unidentified, almost microscopic square seed, with a notch in its edge, possibly some species of birdsfoot trefoil (*Lotus*). Nearly all of the leguminous plants that furnish the quail with seeds belong in the category of weeds.

Seeds of weeds from other families of plants make up no less than

---

[a] Birds of Colorado, App. 2, p. 202, 1900,

41.89 per cent of the annual food. Seeds of compositæ yield 5.55 per cent, such injurious weeds as thistles making up the largest part of this percentage. The thistles most often eaten are *Centaurea meli-*
tensis, C. americana, C. solstitialis, Ma-
riana mariniana, Sonchus sp., and *Car-*
duus sp. *M. mariniana* has the largest seeds. Ninety of these had been eaten by a quail shot by F. E. L. Beal at Hay-wards, Cal., August 15, 1903. The seeds of the bur thistle (*Centaurea melitensis*) are smaller and have a hook at one end and a set of spines like a paint brush at the other. They are, perhaps, most liked of all composite seeds. From 500 to 800 are often eaten at a meal. The destruc-tion of this seed is highly beneficial,

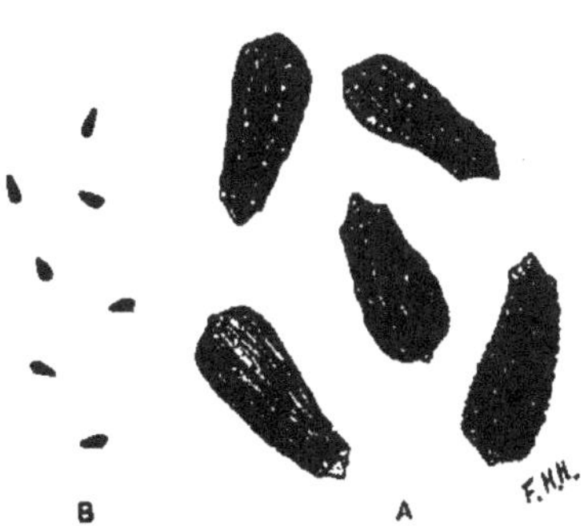

FIG. 4.—Seed of mayweed (*Anthemis cotula*). (From Bull. 38, Nevada Agricultural Experiment Station.)

for the bur thistle is troublesome to farmers. Wild carrot (*Daucus carota*), tar weed (*Madia sativa*), wild lettuce (*Lactuca* sp.), mayweed (*Anthemis cotula*), and marsh elder (*Iva xanthifolia*) furnish most of the remaining seeds of composite plants. Tar weed is a favorite source of food, and one stomach, collected at Watsonville, Cal., by J. S. Hunter, contained 700 of these seeds. Another stomach, from the same place, held 2,000 tiny seeds of dog fennel, or mayweed. (Fig. 4.)

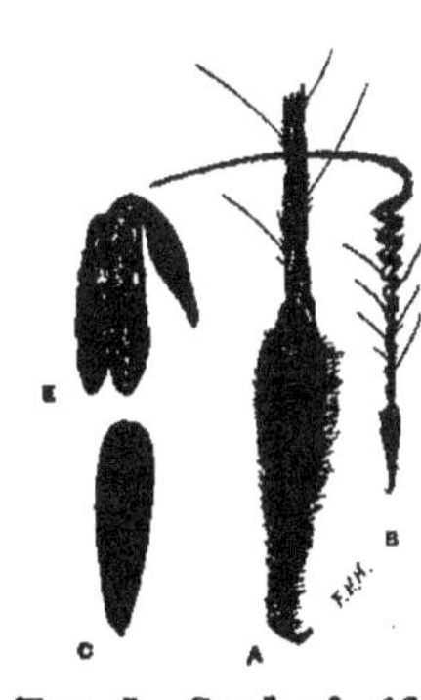

FIG. 5.—Seed of alfilaria (*Erodium cicutarium*). (From Bull. 38, Nevada Agricultural Experiment Station.)

From seeds of plants belonging to the spurge family (*Euphorbiaceæ*) come 5.85 per cent of the annual food. Spurges, particularly *Croton setigerus*, commonly known as turkey mullein, are a staple with the California quail as with most other seed-eating birds. So fond are the quail of turkey mullein that their crops are often completely distended with the seeds, sometimes from 500 to 900 to a bird. Turkey mullein is a prostrate plant covered with a whitish, woolly pubes-cence, and often used by the Indians to poison fish. Seeds of alfilaria (*Erodium cicutarium* and other species), which is both a weed and a forage plant, are eagerly sought. They are lance-shaped, furnished with a long, elaborate,

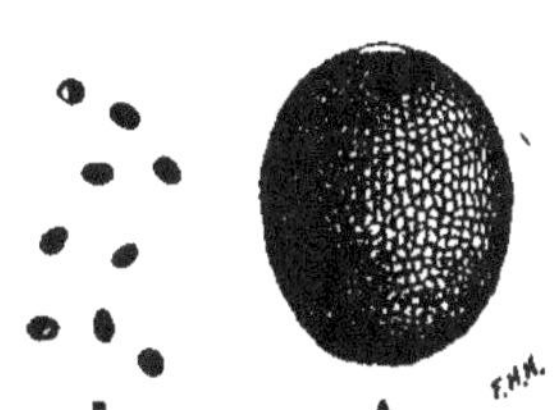

FIG. 6.—Seed of black mustard (*Brassica nigra*). (From Bull. 38, Nevada Agricultural Experiment Station.)

corkscrew awn ending in a thin spine. They burrow into sheep's wool and even pierce the skin. The alfilaria is one of the few seeds of the West that all seed-eating birds consume. The plant is very abundant in California, and the quail often eats from 1,000 to 1,600 of the little corkscrew seeds at a meal. It affords 13.38 per cent of the year's food, and 26.70 per cent of the June diet. (Fig. 5.)

Seeds of miscellaneous weeds comprise 17.11 per cent of the annual food. Among the species included are pigweed (*Chenopodium al-*

FIG. 7.—Seed of chickweed (*Alsine media*). (From Bull. 47, Nevada Agricultural Experiment Station.)

bum), rough pigweed (*Amaranthus retroflexus*), and black mustard (*Brassica nigra*) (fig. 6)—especially obnoxious in grain fields—and the closely related weed, wild radish (*Raphanus sativus*). Seeds of shepherd's purse (*Bursa bursa-pastoris*) and of other cruciferous

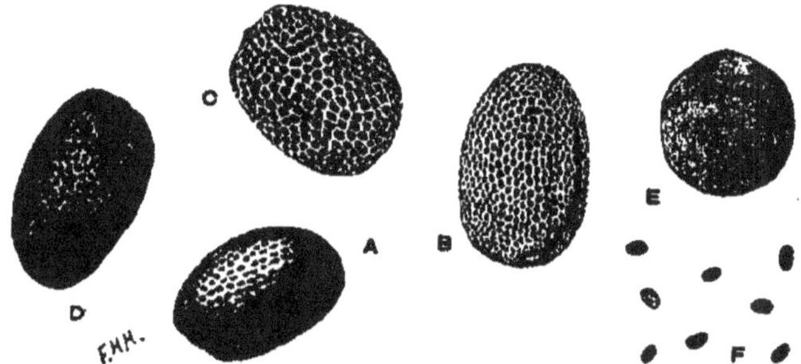

FIG. 8.—Seed of *Geranium dissectum*. (From Bull. 47, Nevada Agricultural Experiment Station.)

plants are included in common with *silene* and the chickweeds (*Cerastium* sp. and *Alsine media*) (fig. 7). Geranium seeds (fig. 8) are so much relished that often 300 or 400 are eaten at a time. Two closely related plants, miner's lettuce (*Montia perfoliata*) and red

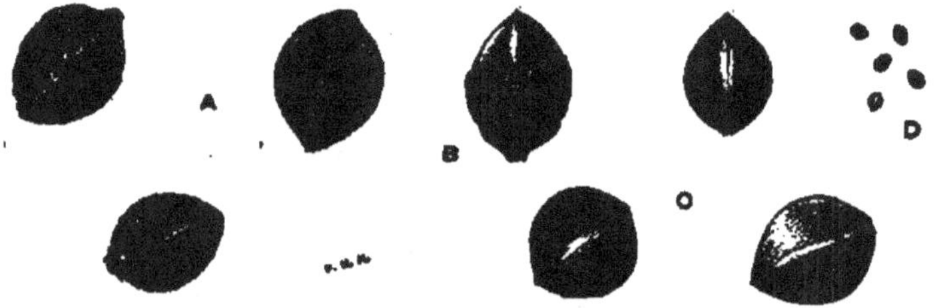

FIG. 9.—Seed of sorrel (*Rumex acetosella*). (From Bull. 47, Nevada Agricultural Experiment Station.)

maids (*Calandrinia menziesii*), bear minute shiny black seeds that often are eaten by the thousand. The little seeds of red sorrel (*Rumex acetosella*) (fig. 9) and curled dock (*Rumex crispus*) are occasionally taken in almost as large numbers. Seeds of chess (*Bromus secalinus* (fig. 10) and *Bromus hordeaceus*), a serious grain pest, are relished, and hundreds of the grain-like seeds of the grass known as 'poison darnel' (*Lolium temulentum*) appear in crops examined. Macoun, quoting Spreadborough, states that in British Columbia, where it winters successfully, the quail finds shelter in severe weather under the broom (*Cytisus scoparius*), which in places grows abundantly and yields seed for subsistence.[a]

The quail feeds also at times on mast. A. K. Fisher, in the western foothills of the Sierra Nevada, the last of July found both young and adult quail eating young acorns.[b] Small quantities of sedge seeds (*Carex* and *Scirpus*) and of dodder (*Cuscuta*) are eaten, the latter plant being a destructive parasite on leguminous forage crops. The miscellaneous seed list includes also stick seeds (*Lappula* sp.), buttercup (*Ranunculus* sp.), bind weed (*Convolvulus* sp.), *Amsinckia* sp., *Anagallis arvensis*, plaintain (*Plantago major*), ribgrass (*Plantago lanceolata*), painted cup (*Castilleja* sp.), mountain lilac

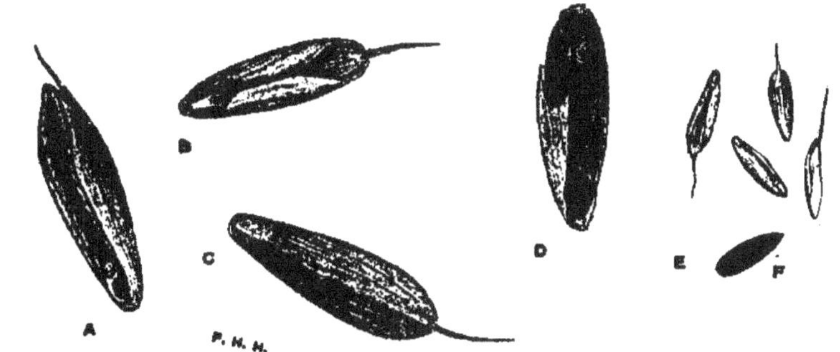

FIG. 10.—Seed of chess (*Bromus secalinus*). (From Bull. 47, Nevada Agricultural Experiment Station.)

(*Ceanothus* sp.), and black wattle (*Callicoma serratifolia*). In the mountains of Lower California the food supply determines the breeding time of birds. If there is not enough rain for a good supply of seeds the coveys of quail do not break up into nesting pairs but remain in coveys throughout the summer. If the season is wet and the winter rains promise abundant food the birds mate in March and begin nesting immediately.[c]

FOOD OF THE YOUNG.

The food of young birds differs from that of the parents, as has already been remarked of the bobwhite, but the difference is less marked with the California quail. Stomachs of 32 young of the western birds, from one-fourth to one-half grown, have been examined. They were collected from the middle of July to the middle of September. The food was composed of 3.4 per cent animal matter

a Cat. Can. Birds, Part I, p. 198, 1900.

b N. A. Fauna, No. 7, p. 28, 1893.

c Life Hist. N. A. Birds [I], p. 27, 1892.

and 96.6 per cent vegetable matter. Thirty-nine adult birds shot in the same period had eaten almost entirely vegetable food, since only 0.6 per cent of animal food appeared in analysis. Had the young birds been collected when newly hatched, undoubtedly a larger proportion of insect food would have been found. The 3.4 per cent of insect food mentioned consisted of beetles, 0.1 per cent; bugs, 0.2 per cent; grasshoppers, 1.3 per cent, and ants, 1.8 per cent.

The vegetable food of the young is much like that of the adult. In this case it consisted of leguminous seeds, 18.1 per cent; alfilaria seeds, 18.5 per cent; miscellaneous seeds, 54.4 per cent; browse, 6.6 per cent; grain, 0.6 per cent, and miscellaneous vegetable matter, 0.4 per cent.

GAMBEL QUAIL.

(*Lophortyx gambeli.*)

[PLATE II.]

The Gambel quail in general appearance is much like the valley quail, but, among other differences, lacks the scalelike feathers of the lower parts and has considerable chestnut along the flanks. It lives in the Lower Sonoran zone, from western Texas to southeastern California and from southern Utah and Nevada south through central Sonora, Mexico. The desert is its home, but it is rarely found far from water. Its favorite haunts are patches of bushy vegetation, such as mesquite, mimosa, creosote, and patches of prickly pear. It frequently takes up its abode about cultivated land, living in alfalfa fields or nesting in vineyards.

An interesting account of the habits of the Gambel quail in the Pahrump Valley, Nevada, is given by E. W. Nelson:

I noticed that when a flock of quail came to feed on grain left by the horses an old male usually mounted the top of a tall bush close by and remained on guard for ten or fifteen minutes; then, if everything was quiet, he would fly down among his companions. At the first alarm the flock would take to the bushes, running swiftly, or flying when hard pressed. They roosted in the dense bunches of willows and cottonwoods growing along the ditches. * * * When feeding they have a series of low clucking and cooing notes which are kept up almost continually.[a]

The love note, according to Coues, may be represented in words as 'killink, killink.' Nesting takes place in April, sometimes not till May. About a dozen eggs usually constitute a clutch. In sections where this quail is still numerous the birds *pack* in bands of from 100 to 500 after the breeding season.

From the sportsman's point of view the Gambel quail as a game bird does not approach the bobwhite. It will sometimes lie to a dog

---

[a] N. A. Fauna, No. 7, pp. 29, 30, 1893.

GAMBEL QUAIL (LOPHORTYX GAMBELI).

fairly well, but as a rule it takes to its legs with all haste and leaves the dog on point, to the vexation of the hunter. It is, however, a useful species, which brightens the desert with its presence and contributes a welcome addition to the fare of the traveler. While less valuable than the bobwhite as a destroyer of noxious insects and as an object of sport, this bird well deserves protection for its food value and its beauty. It thrives under desert conditions and might be successfully introduced in the arid regions of Colorado, New Mexico, and Texas.

FOOD HABITS.

Stomachs of 28 birds collected mainly in Arizona and Utah, from January to June, have been examined. Only 0.48 per cent of the food consisted of insects; the remaining 99.52 per cent was vegetable matter. Like the valley quail, this is one of our least insectivorous birds. Its insect diet includes ants, beetles, grasshoppers, leaf hoppers (*Membracidæ*), and stink bugs (*Pentatomidæ*). Among the beetles are the western twelve-spotted cucumber beetle (*Diabrotica soror*) and *D. tenella*. The young chicks, however, will doubtless be found highly insectivorous and therefore useful.

The vegetable food of Gambel quail was made up as follows: Grain, 3.89 per cent, miscellaneous seeds, 31.89 per cent, and leaves and plant shoots, 63.74 per cent. From the present investigation the bird appears less frugivorous than any of the other American quails, for not one of the 28 stomachs contained fruit. Observers, however, say that the bird is somewhat frugivorous, and no doubt in a country well stocked with berries and fruit it would rapidly develop a frugivorous taste. Baird, Brewer, and Ridgway, for instance, state that during summer it makes its home in patches of *Solanum* and feeds on the tolerably palatable fruit, and also that it is known to eat gooseberries.[a] Coues says: "In the fall it gathers cherries and grapes. * * * It visits patches of prickly pear (*Opuntia*) to feed upon the soft juicy 'Tunas' that are eaten by everything in Arizona, from men and bears to beetles."[b]

The grain eaten by the Gambel quail was corn, wheat, and oats. In flocks numbering from 50 to 100, it feeds about grain stacks with domestic poultry. It is even more industrious as a browser on foliage than the valley quail. Succulent foliage and shoots form 63.74 per cent of its food. Much of this comes from alfalfa, bur clover, and the foliage of other legumes. Vernon Bailey, of the Biological Survey, says that at St. Thomas, Ariz., in January, 1889, this quail fairly swarmed on alfalfa fields, feeding on the green leaves and pods. He found flocks of from 25 to 50 in such situations, and during a

---

[a] Birds of Northwest, p. 434, 1874.　　[b] Hist. N. Am. Birds, III, p. 483, 1874.

five minutes' walk often saw a hundred birds. The same observer, when in Mohave County, Ariz., found that the bird fed principally on juicy plants when it could not procure water. At times it eats grass and its inflorescence, and it has been known to devour showy flowers. In spring it shows a fondness for buds. Baird, Brewer, and Ridgway note that then it feeds largely on the willow buds, which impart to its flesh a distinctly bitter taste.[a]

The seed-eating habits of Gambel quail closely resemble those of the valley quail. Leguminous plants furnish the largest part of the seed food—21.17 per cent of the annual diet—alfalfa, bur clover, and kindred plants appearing to be preferred, but cassias, acacias, and lupines also are taken, as well as the beans of the mesquite, which in many places are a staple with birds and mammals. The seeds of alfilaria (*Erodium cicutarium*), another bird staple, furnish 2.28 per cent of the year's food. Miscellaneous seeds form 8.44 per cent. They are obtained from grasses, mallows (*Malva*), and such cruciferous plants as mustard (*Brassica*) and peppergrass (*Lepidium*); also from chickweed (*Cerastium*) and *Atriplex*.

MOUNTAIN QUAIL.

(*Oreortyx pictus.*[b])

The mountain quail occurs in the forested mountains of the humid Transition Zone of the Pacific coast, from Santa Barbara, Cal., to Washington, and in the mountains of the more arid Transition Zone on the west side of the Cascades in northern Oregeon and south over the Sierra Nevada to northern Lower California. The birds of the Sierra Nevada winter at lower altitudes than they nest, but those of the coast mountains do not make this vertical migration. This species is the largest and among the handsomest of American quail, with two long jet-black crest plumes and rich chestnut throat and flanks, the latter broadly banded transversely with spotless white.

The nests of the mountain quail are placed on the ground and usually contain 10 to 12 eggs, which vary from pale-cream color to a much darker due. At Tillamook, Oreg., June 30 and July 4, 1897, A. K. Fisher found newly hatched chicks; and at Donner, Cal., July 11 and 19, at an altitude ranging from 6,100 to 8,000 feet, Vernon Bailey found nine broods, varying in age from newly hatched chicks to half-grown birds. Bendire, quoting L. W. Green, of the United States Fish Commission, says that the earliest date of the nesting of

---

[a] Hist. N. Am. Birds, III, p. 485, 1874.

[b] The name is used here to cover both the typical dark birds of the humid coast forests (*Oreortyx pictus*) and the paler one (*O. p. plumiferus*) of the more arid Transition Zone in the Sierras and Cascades.

the plumed mountain quail (*Oreortyx p. plumiferus*) known to him was April 15, and the latest, August 15. He states also that the cock bird takes care of the young.[a] Chester Barlow, in writing of the habits of the mountain quail, says that at Fyffe, Cal., it begins to nest the last of May or early in June. All nests that he found were built in a growth of ' mountain misery ' (*Chamæbatia* sp.) 8 to 10 inches high.[b] On Mount Tallac and the higher slopes of Pyramid Peak, W. W. Price found newly hatched young as late as August 15. He noted that by September 1 the quail became restless and soon began their peculiar migration from the east slope to the west slope of the Sierras. From 4 to 6 adults with their young form a small band of from 10 to 30 individuals, and pursue their way almost wholly on foot to a more congenial winter climate; and by October 1 all had abandoned elevations above 5,000 feet. In spring they migrate back singly or in pairs.[c]

There are many admirers of this bird because of its exquisite plumage, but most sportsmen prefer a game bird that lies better to the dog. Its flesh is excellent, and the bird sells well in the market. H. W. Henshaw reports that in the late fall of 1880 he found the markets of Portland, Oreg., well supplied with live mountain quails which had been trapped in the neighboring mountains, cooped, and sent to the city for sale. Nowhere is it so numerous as the California quail, or the bobwhite in the Southern States, and it is more of a forest-loving species than any other American quail. The mountain quail sometimes enters cleared fields, but so far as the records of the Biological Survey show it does no appreciable damage to cultivated fruits or other crops and it is a useful destroyer of weed seeds.

FOOD HABITS.

No stomachs of the mountain quail of the humid regions were available for examination, but Sandys writes that the bird feeds on insects and various seeds, including grain,[d] and Elliot says it sometimes approaches farm buildings in search of scattered kernels of grain.[e]

The food of the mountain quail of the arid regions has been studied in the laboratory of the Biological Survey. The stomachs examined, 23 in number, were collected in California. Five were collected in January, 2 in May, 6 in June, 3 in July, 3 in August, and

<hr>

a Life Hist. N. Am. Birds [I], p. 16, 1892.
b Condor, 3, p. 158, 1901.
c Condor, 3, pp. 158, 160, 1901.
d Upland Game Birds, p. 93, 1902.
e Gallinaceous Game Birds N. A., p. 42, 1897.

6 in November. The food consisted of animal matter, 3 per cent, and vegetable matter, 97 per cent. The animal food was made up of grasshoppers, 0.05 per cent; beetles, 0.23 per cent; miscellaneous insects, including ants and lepidopterous pupæ, 1.90 per cent; and centipedes and harvest spiders (*Phalangidæ*), 0.82 per cent. Among the beetles was a species of the firefly family (*Lampyridæ*), a ground beetle (*Carabidæ*), and a leaf beetle (*Haltica* sp.). Vernon Bailey informs the writer that the young eat many ants. The vegetable food consisted of grain, 18.20 per cent; seeds, practically all of weeds or other worthless plants, 46.61 per cent; fruit, 8.11 per cent; and miscellaneous vegetable matter, 24.08 per cent. The grain included wheat, corn, barley, and oats. Of the seed element the seeds of grasses formed 7.78 per cent; of legumes, 10.41 per cent; of weeds of the family *Euphorbiaceæ*, 3.16 per cent; of alfilaria (*Erodium cicutarium*), 2.76 per cent; and of miscellaneous weeds, 22.50 per cent. The legume seeds include seeds of alfalfa, cassia, bush clover, vetch, and lupine. The miscellaneous seeds come from wild carrot (*Daucus carota*), tar weed (*Madia sativa*), *Collomia* sp., *Amsinckia* sp., labiate plants, dwarf oak, snowbush (*Ceanothus cordulatus*), and thistle.

Concerning the feeding habits of mountain quail of the dry country (*O. p. plumiferus*), J. E. McClellan says: "Their feeding hours are early in the morning and just before sundown in the evening, when they go to roost in the thick tops of the scrub live oaks. Their feeding habits are similar to those of the domestic hen. They are vigorous scratchers, and will jump a foot or more from the ground to nip off leaves."[a] This bird is especially fond of the leaves of clover and other leguminous plants. It feeds also on flowers, being known to select those of Compositæ and blue-eyed grass (*Sisyrinchium*). Flowers, leaves, buds, and other kinds of vegetable matter form the 24.08 per cent marked miscellaneous. The birds probably eat more fruit than these stomach examinations indicate. Lyman Belding says that this quail feeds on service berries, and that during certain seasons it lives almost entirely on grass bulbs (*Melica bulbosa*), which it gets by scratching, for which its large, powerful feet are well adapted. The fruit in its bill of fare includes gooseberries, service berries (*Amelanchier alnifolia*), and grapes (*Vitis californica*). The bird is probably fond also of manzanita berries, for it is often seen among these shrubs.

---

[a] MS. Records, Biological Survey.

SCALED QUAIL.

(*Callipepla squamata.*)[a]

The 'cotton top,' or scaled quail, as it is commonly known, is bluish gray on the back, with black-edged feathers on the under parts, which appear like large scales. Its conspicuous white-tipped crest has given it the local name of cotton top. It is found in southern Colorado and in the Upper and Lower Sonoran zones from Arizona to western and southern Texas and south to the Valley of Mexico. The birds of the lower Rio Grande region are darker than those farther west. According to Bendire, this quail lives on open arid plains overgrown with yucca, cactus, and sagebrush, and often gathers in coveys numbering 25 to 80. It lays about a dozen eggs, and he believes that two or three broods are reared in a season. The cock assists in the care of the young, but not in incubation.[b]

FOOD HABITS.

The food habits of this game bird are of especial interest. Stomachs and crops of 47 specimens have been examined, most of which came from New Mexico, the others from Arizona and Texas. They were collected as follows: January, 7; May, 1; June, 2; July, 3; September, 13; October, 19, and November, 2. As with all other gallinaceous birds, more or less mineral matter is swallowed, usually small pieces of quartz. The food consisted of animal matter, 29.6 per cent, and vegetable matter, 70.4 per cent.

The food of the cotton top differs from that of all other American quails in that it contains a large proportion of insects. These comprise no less than 29.03 per cent of its food, a percentage almost twice as great as that of the bobwhite, although if more stomachs of the present species had been available for examination the ratio might have been different. However, the important fact is established that this bird is a large consumer of insects, instead of being, like most other western quail, practically graminivorous. Of the insect food, grasshoppers comprise 15.86 per cent; beetles, 10.43 per cent, and miscellaneous insects, largely ants, 3.27 per cent. A few spiders also are taken, but they constitute only 0.03 per cent of the food for the year. The beetles are in the larval as well as the adult forms. The family of ground beetles (*Carabidæ*), a favorite one with terrestrial birds, is well represented. A single beetle with a featherlike antenna, of the family *Pyrochroidæ*, had been eaten. Some longicorn beetles and plant-eating scarabæid beetles also were eaten. A bird collected in

---

[a] The name of the species is used here to include both the typical scaled quail (*Callipepla squamata*) and the more restricted chestnut-bellied quail of southern Texas (*C. s. castanogastris*).

[b] Life Hist. N. A. Birds [I], pp. 18–20, 1892.

June had consumed 44 of the latter beetles, which were leaf chafers, apparently closely related to the genus *Serica*. The scaled quail destroys also weevils, such as the clover weevil, *Sitones*, and certain species of the family *Otiorhynchidæ*, or scarred snout beetles. It takes also leaf beetles, the very injurious twelve-spotted cucumber beetle (*Diabrotica 12-punctata*). Further studies of the beetle food undoubtedly will disclose a large number of pests. The bird will probably be found to be a useful consumer also of grasshoppers, since a third of its September food consisted of them. Their remains were so fragmentary, however, that identification of species was unsatisfactory. In one case a member of the genus *Trimerotropis* was recognized. Ants had been eaten by 15 of the 47 birds examined. The other miscellaneous insects included small bugs (*Heteroptera*) and the chrysalis of a fly. One of the queerest objects found by the writer in birds' stomachs is the 'ground pearl' (*Margarodes*), several hundred of which were contained in the stomach of a cotton top shot at Roswell, N. Mex., June 17, 1899. They are lustrous and look like pearls, but are merely scale insects that feed on the roots of plants.

Vegetable matter furnished 70 per cent of the food of the scaled quail. Grain contributed 0.57 per cent; seeds, mostly weed seeds, 52.85 per cent; fruit, 12.65 per cent, and leaves and other green tissue, 4.33 per cent. The species resembles the ruffed grouse in its habit of feeding on green leaves and tender shoots. It feeds upon budded twigs, but more often limits its choice to chlorophyll-bearing tissue, often picking green seed pods of various plants. Like domestic fowls, it eats grass blades. Fruit was eaten by only 6 of the 47 birds, and none was taken from cultivated varieties. As might be expected from inhabitants of arid plains, these birds like the fruit of cacti, and have been found feeding on the prickly pear (*Opuntia lindheimeri*). The fruit of *Ibervillea lindheimeri* also is eaten. The blue berries of *Adelia angustifolia*, which furnish many desert birds and mammals with food, are often eaten by the scaled quail. Different kinds of *Rubus* fruits are relished, and the berries of *Koeberlinia spinosa* and *Momisia pallida* also are eaten. The fruit and succulent parts of plants no doubt serve in part in the parched desert as a substitute for water.

Seeds of various plants form a little more than half of the food. Legumes furnish 21.84 per cent, the mesquite (*Prosopis juliflora*), a staple with both man and beast, being utilized, as are the seeds of mimosa (*M. biuncifera*), besides various cassias and lupines. Seeds of vetch (*Vicia* sp.) are a favorite food, and *Morongia roemeriana* is eaten. The bird likes seeds of *Medicago*, and at times will eat clover seeds. Miscellaneous weed seeds yield 31.01 per cent of the annual food. Nearly half of these are seeds of bindweed (*Convolvulus* sp.), an abundant and troublesome weed in the South, where it often throttles other plants. The following miscellaneous seeds were found among their food:

Thistle (*Carduus* sp.).
Wild sunflower (*Helianthus annuus*).
Coreopsis (*Coreopsis coronaria*).
Aster (*Aster* sp.).
Chamomile (*Anthemis* sp.).
Pigweed (*Amaranthus* sp.).
Gromwell (*Lithospermum* sp.).

Borage (*Amsinckia* sp.).
Mallow (*Malva rotundifolia*).
Turkey mullein (*Croton setigerus*).
Croton (*Croton texensis*).
Alfilaria (*Erodium cicutarium*).
Spurge (*Euphorbia* sp.).

Grass seeds have not yet been found in quantity in the crop of the species, but panicum seeds have been recognized.

In summing up the economic status of the scaled quail it should be noted that although the bird is a desert species, it comes into more or less direct relation with agriculture, sometimes feeding upon cultivated land and about farm buildings. Moreover, half of its food consists of the seeds of weeds. Lastly, it is highly insectivorous, fully one-fourth of its food consisting of insects.

MEARNS QUAIL.

(*Cyrtonyx montezumæ mearnsi.*[a])

The pervading colors of the male Mearns quail are black, white, and chestnut. Its thick speckles of white and its peculiar shape suggest a miniature guinea hen. The species is found on the table-lands of Mexico from the City of Mexico north to western Texas, New Mexico, and Arizona, but the bird considered here is limited to the northern part of this range.

It is a confiding bird and either from excess of curiosity or from stupidity has been known to remain on the ground to be killed by a stick. From this lack of suspicion it has received the name ' fool quail.' It affords the sportsman with a dog much better shooting than its more erratic crested relatives. Grassy or bushy cover is more necessary to this bird than to the scaled quail or Gambel quail. Unlike the latter species, it does not pack, though it is more or less migratory. Its nesting habits are not well known. Bendire describes a nest found in Kinney County, Tex., June 22, 1890. It was placed in a depression of the ground, and contained 10 eggs.

FOOD HABITS.

The food habits of the Mearns quail are not well known. The Biological Survey has examined the contents of 9 crops and stom-

[a] The typical Massena quail (*Cyrtonyx montezuma*) is a bird of the mountains about the Mexican table-land, and gives way to the paler Mearns quail (*C. m. mearnsi*) in northern Mexico and the southwestern United States.

achs, secured in Texas and New Mexico during August and November. Two of the birds were killed in a patch of cactus. They contained seeds and spines from the prickly pear, acacia, and other seeds, grass blades, and a trace of insects—weevils and other beetles—besides a large quantity of coarse sand and iron ore. The other 7 birds were shot in August. Two had their crops filled with the bulbs of a lily. The others also had eaten lily bulbs, which in the 5 birds made three-fourths of the food. The other food was prickly pear fruit, seeds of legumes and spurges, and such insects as weevils, smooth caterpillars, hairy caterpillars, bugs, crickets, and grasshoppers. Cassin states that the contents of the crop of a specimen sent him from Texas by Captain French " consisted exclusively of fragments of insects, pronounced by Doctor Leconte to be principally grasshoppers and a specimen of *Spectrum*." [a] According to Baird, Brewer, and Ridgway, the Mearns quail appeared quite at home in cultivated fields and stubble of the ranches.[b] Away from civilization it prefers districts covered with open forest, with alternate areas of grass and scattered bushy undergrowth, or hillsides covered with grass and bushes. Its habits vary considerably with the locality. Bendire records that the species lives in rocky ravines and arroyos, but quickly adapts itself to ranch conditions and may be seen running about to gather kernels of scattered grain. He says also that it is fond of acorns, mountain laurel, arbutus, cedar, and other berries, and notes that its large, strong feet are well suited to unearthing the bulbs on which it feeds. He found holes 2 inches deep which it had dug for this purpose. These quail often come out into mountain roads to search for scattered grain and to dust themselves. As they are readily tamed, they could doubtless be successfully introduced into other regions.

---

[a] Illustration of Birds of California, Texas, etc., p. 25, 1856.
[b] Hist. N. Am. Birds, III, p. 492, 1874.